Endorsements from Ministry

I found Dr. Antonia M. Arnold-McFarland's book entitled *Moving Forward and Facing the Future* an exhaustive contribution of enlightenment in regard to the Black Church worship experience.

This offering is inspiring, exhilarating, and extremely necessary to advance the evolution of gospel music tradition. McFarland's stellar publication will provide a treasure trove of information in regard to the history of African-American sacred music, the establishment of biblical music ministry, and the root challenges of music and worship arts ministry of today's church. Her wonderfully written manuscript will empower senior pastors, worship pastors, worship leaders, ministers of music, music directors, music administrators, music ministry instructors, singers, and musicians to obtain deliberate and invigorating education on how to develop and maintain excellence in the music worship ministry.

Additionally, this book provides answers to solve problems many encounter in church music ministry infrastructure and leadership.

Steven Ford, Ph.D.
Grammy Award Producer, Orchestrator, Educator, and Lecturer
Author of *Is Your Music Department Ministry or Misery?*
Middletown, DE

* * *

Excellence personified! An appropriate term to describe the music genius of Dr. Antonia M. Arnold-McFarland. She is an accomplished teacher, director, coach, and clinician with church choirs, praise teams, and other musical ensembles. For a period of approximately eight years, Dr. McFarland transformed the music ministry at Oak City Baptist Church from average or mediocre to one of excellence by using the principles contained in this guide. This much needed document for improving the music and worship arts ministry in churches has my highest recommendation!

Rev. Dr. William T. Newkirk Sr.
Senior Pastor
Oak City Baptist Church, Raleigh, NC

* * *

Dr. Antonia M. Arnold-McFarland's *Moving Forward and Facing the Future in The Black Church Worship Experience* is a significant contribution to the resources offered to Christians seeking to live a more meaningful, worshipful, and purposeful life. Dr. Arnold-McFarland has given us a book that represents the journey to the sacred well that she has personally drawn from throughout the breadth and depth of her own effective ministry as a worship coach and a private devotee of Jesus Christ.

Our friend of 20 years, affectionately known as Toni, has provided a road map for ministry leaders that tells us where to go and how to get to the center of worship. Although this masterpiece focuses on music and worship, the benefits transcend all facets of church ministry. This practical guide has transformed our entire ministry and will continue to edify our future development. Having had the firsthand experience of Dr. Arnold-McFarland as our resident worship consultant, we highly recommend her consultation services and her practical guide as a must have.

Pastor-Teacher George M. Greene and Lady Kerri Greene
Christian Home Christian Church, Apex, NC

* * *

Dr. Antonia M. Arnold-McFarland has a pulse that vibrates the very arteries of music and worship arts in the Black Church. Her pulse on the subject encourages all of us to serve with the utmost confidence in the area of church music. Music and worship art continues to shape us as we evolve in our theology.

Elder Roland Perry, National Gospel Songwriter
Author, *The African-American Church Musician's Compensation and Salary Handbook*
Minister of Music, North East Baptist Church, Durham, NC

* * *

An African proverb intimates that "the Spirit cannot descend without a song." So it remains the case for the black churches and the black worship experience today. Dr. Antonia Arnold-McFarland has written a powerful volume that speaks to the contemporary needs and future prospects of music and worship arts ministry in the Black Church. Through exhaustive scholarly research and grounded in her vast experience as a practitioner in the areas of worship leadership and choral direction, Dr. Arnold-McFarland addresses many of the dynamics that will affect the black worship experience into the future, and she offers prescriptive, practical insight as to how worship experiences can be enhanced in years to come. Her work is must read material for church and worship leaders serving in Black Church contexts.

C. Anthony Hunt, Ph.D.
Professor and Distinguished Lecturer of Theology, St. May's Seminary and University, Baltimore, MD Author of *Keep Looking Up: Sermons on the Psalms*
Senior Pastor, Epworth Chapel United Methodist Church, Baltimore, MD

* * *

Dr. Antonia Arnold-McFarland's expertise in the area of music and worship arts in the Black Church, coupled with her innovative approach to the subject, identifies her as an unparalleled leader in this field. Dr. Arnold-McFarland has a data-driven, quantitative understanding of her field, which she is able to effortlessly integrate into the praxis aspects of daily music ministry. This book will most certainly become the go-to text for all those individuals engaged in music ministry in the Black Church.

Kendra E. Clayton, Ed.D.
President, Graduate Theological Foundation, Mishawaka, IN

* * *

Dr. Antonia M. Arnold-McFarland,

You are a jewel and blessing to me. I am thankful that our paths have crossed, and I thank you for your wisdom, guidance, understanding, and friendship. You are a true visionary thinker and a gospel music genre expert. You have encouraged me, many times without even knowing it, to press on during an unfavorable situation. We at Eastern Carolina Christian College and Seminary are grateful to have you as an adjunct professor who offers research expertise and vast knowledge in worship and gospel music.

Always grateful.

Reverend Dr. Jean D. Brown
President, Dissertation, Thesis, Resource, and Services (D.T.R.S.)
Vice President, Academics and Faculty at Eastern
Carolina Christian College & Seminary
Associate Minister, Oak City Baptist Church, Raleigh, NC

* * *

Anyone involved in the music and worship arts ministry of the Black Church will treasure this book. From cover to cover, Dr. Antonia Arnold-McFarland addresses critical issues that have long concerned those of us in church music ministry. This book provides information on how music started in the Black Church and challenges us to be creative in maintaining its purpose.

Dona Jackson Anderson
Producer, WRAL-TV's *Spiritual Awakening*
President, New Beginnings Entertainment
Music Ministry, Oak City Baptist Church, Raleigh, NC

* * *

Music has been and will always be an integral part of the worship experience. Worship is at the core of everything the church does. Worship must be exciting, innovating, refreshing, relevant, and hopeful. Over the last decade, the "church" has undergone transition by choice and by demand, facing difficult challenges that speak to purposeful worship rather than worthless rituals. Dr. Arnold-McFarland is a woman who has committed her music passion through serving and preparing the church to meet the needs through holistic worship. I have personally witnessed her growth over the years and have felt her heart to serve, educate, and inspire others.

Minister Thomas Vanhook Jr., Principal Consultant
Vocal Inspiration, Church Leadership Consulting
White Rock Baptist Church, Durham, NC

* * *

I have known "Toni" for 25 years from working together in various groups and music activities. As a vocalist in Blessed Union, The Group, our work together has given me the opportunity to record with industry recognized producers, to sing lead on released singles, to learn the music industry, to be fed spiritually through ministry advisors, to study voice with exceptional instructors, to perform at the I Am Radio New Artist Showcase (Stellar Awards Weekend), and to see how connections create possibilities. We have traveled locally and from state-to-state on various music venues, where I was able to understand the sacrifice, hard work, and creativity required to obtain a professional production, performance, and presentation. We have enjoyed a bond that goes beyond music. Her passion for helping people often is evident in her witness, even when music is not the focus of the connection. This book pulls all these experiences together and shows ministry leaders how to bring the best out of people.

Elder Vicki Thomas, Vocalist and Psalmist
Pursuing His Highest Ministries, Garner, NC
True Way Holiness Church, Raleigh, NC

* * *

For hundreds of years African-Americans have practiced and sustained a unique pattern of worship. The energy and passion found within their worship has proven to be both an amazement and anomaly to those inside and outside of the African-American tradition. Yet the process of worship has transformed as much as it has been a transforming agent among African-Americans. Dr. Antonia addresses the evolution of African-American worship from the days of slavery through to the 21st century. By applying quantitative and qualitative methods of research she helps to provide an explanation for the energy, freedom of expression, and evolution of the African-American worship experience. Through assessment and analysis of the historical evolution of African-American worship, Dr. Antonia has been able to offer insight and suggest practical measures for improving and sustaining this rich cultural tradition of worship.

Raymond Wise, Ph.D.
Professor of Practice, African-American and African Diaspora Studies
Indiana University, Bloomington, IN
President, Raise Productions Center for the Gospel Arts

Moving Forward and Facing the Future by Dr. Antonia M. Arnold-McFarland

Editing services by ChristianEditingServices.com

Cover and Interior Design by dhbonner.net

ISBN: 978-1-7323365-0-6

Gospel Music One Sound Project Presents

Moving Forward *and* Facing the Future

In the Black Church Worship Experience

Dr. Antonia M. Arnold-McFarland

DEDICATION

To my parents, Raymond T. Arnold Jr.
and the late Mary F. Arnold.

Thank you for encouraging me to grow spiritually,
academically, and musically.

Your sacrifices, teaching, and modeling have been invaluable.

CONTENTS

Appendices

FOREWORD

The influence of black gospel music on the Black Church has been nothing more than revolutionary. In fact, some would say they are one and the same. The soul, emotion, and revelation embodied in the music has been one of the foundational pillars for perfection, edifying and unifying African-Americans for many years. In fact, music has always been an integral part of our worship to God. From the song of Moses, to David's psalms, to the admonishing by the apostle to sing spiritual songs unto the Lord, music has always been and will forevermore play a major part in our worship.

It is almost unthinkable that in this day and time, many denominations have devalued the institution of music and have sought to hinder its growth and effectiveness in our worship experience. Nothing has become more real to me than this since I've been pastoring: A great song will find itself into the heart of more people faster than the preached Word will. This is not to devalue the supremacy of the preached Word. God forbid. But this revelation is given to open our eyes to this fact: People remember the words of a great song more than they remember the most eloquent sermons. Now if that song is rooted in sound biblical doctrine, it can change the world. It will get into places that a preached word cannot. I am not biased toward either because both gifts rest within me. However, I do recognize the need to continue to educate the body concerning this ministry we call music.

The Bible exposes the power of music through many extraordinary examples. Through the witness of King Jehoshaphat's choir we see a mighty tool of war. In the melodies of David we see an anti-depression agent. In the dedication of Solomon's temple, we see the ushering in of such a great presence of God that it rendered the priest motionless. These are all documented examples of the power that God affords us through music.

With this power available to the local church, one must wonder why our gatherings lack the demonstration we see in Scripture. In many cases, music is nothing more than a brief intermission of what some call a "worship" service. The power and the full benefit available to us through this institution is never completely realized.

We are living in a time when there is a great need for the manifested power of God in every area of our lives. This is the dispensation of the church or what theologians call the church age. The church is God's plan for the world's problems. It is a teaching institution. More than any other time in history, the stage is set for God's people to return to a position of authority and leadership with the aroma of the presence of the Sovereign Lord on us. Recognizing music and its power in our worship will energize, empower, and elevate our efforts to establish and grow the kingdom on earth.

I have often wondered how divisions and fractions exist in monumental proportions within our local church music departments. We are called to make the God of the Bible a reality to those who have not witnessed Him. Our music ministries should be so potent that in our worship service, healing and deliverance could take place prior to the preached Word. The manifested power of music should produce countless victories and testimonies in the midst of our worship. In many cases, we leave our worship services in an emotional frenzy, with the absence of life-changing demonstration.

I noted earlier that music is a powerful weapon of warfare. The confidence King Jehoshaphat had in his choir speaks volumes concerning the power of music. What leader would send a choir as the front line of defense into a war? Think about it. He used melody and harmony in place of guns and missiles! To most, this is unthinkable, to say the least. It takes a leader who is intimately involved with God to know the power of authentic praise. Only one who has a true relationship with God understands that touching His heart causes Him to move. You know the story: Jehoshaphat sent his choir before his army and the enemy was confused by the praise that arose before them. Praise will still confuse your enemy.

How many battles have we lost because authentic praise did not precede our fight? For many years I have served pastors, assisting them in building their music ministries. In many cases defeat and depression loomed within those ministries, and the very tool to resurrect the environment was viewed with little importance. Like a voice crying in the wilderness, I pleaded with those pastors and explained that God's plan was to arm their local church music ministry to wage war in the atmosphere. I wonder how many church meetings, board debates, and mutinies could have been avoided with praise preceding every battle.

Some years ago while I was conducting a series of workshops, the Spirit of the Lord showed me yet more problems hindering the power of the local church music ministry. As I began to teach, the spirit of freedom and creativity began to arise. The praise began to increase, and the flow of the anointing was present in such a mighty way. *Wow,* I thought, *this is awesome and just what God desires.* Much to my surprise I was told later that the pastor of that church had issues with this flow of worship. I inquired further about his concerns, only to find that what he desired was a more restricted worship environment. He wanted his worship service to be controlled and dictated. Ironically, I so happened to be teaching from 2 Chronicles 5, which tells that the praise was so great the priest could not stand to minister.

Unfortunately, in the church where the pastor had issues with the flow of worship, I learned there *was* a power present every Sunday, but it was being suppressed and controlled. Because of the absence of the power of praise, many depressing and defeated concepts entered that house. What a tragedy! The goal of every praise team and choir should be to sing such that the anointing becomes so great that God interrupts with His own agenda. I have seen this same dynamic many times over since this experience; the power of praise is present yet unrealized.

For this reason, I have imparted my experiences in symposiums and workshops and on panels to preach and teach the importance of effective worship as it is conducive in healing the broken, which is the purpose and calling of my life ministry work. I have mentored and partnered with many exceptionally talented, astute, and anointed people in my 25-year career. None, however, have been greater than the author of this much needed book. In 2006, while being contracted for a theater production in Durham, North Carolina, I met a young lady who was eager to maximize her gifts, knowledge, and abilities to advance music ministry extensively. As a result of our acquaintance, I began mentoring her and her husband on their pursuit of the music industry as the founders of their own group.

During the process of mentoring and sharing ministry and industry experiences, I became aware of her unique skill set. As an engineer by profession (which is an exact science), she was able to recognize instantly the discipline and commitment required to build a ministry. Having the ability to attain excellence in her craft while pursuing excellence in relationship with God made her unique. I soon began sharing critical ideas and concepts with her concerning church planting. As a result of her thirst for growth and knowledge, she quickly established herself as an essential administrative part of my church and my music ministry and later a resource to my industry activities. After working with her in this capacity for over 10 years, I have realized that she knows not only how to identify and isolate problems but also how to offer multiple solutions to proactively solve those problems.

For these reasons, she can transfer her skills to address music ministry issues in strategy and execution. Her book is a necessary read to the modern pastor. Today pastors are faced with the church's loss of gifts to secular music, the high turnover rate of musicians, commercialization of church worship, and the lack of creativity because of industry dependence of the local church music ministry. These problems require rigorous examination to identify deep-rooted issues.

The ideas and concepts this book embodies have been carefully dissected and supported by qualitative and quantitative data, research studies, and field experiences from an engineering perspective. It contains both critical and creative solutions to common problems we face in music ministry today. These solutions and best practices have been applied and supported with demonstrated results. The book provides the steps to transformation in a way that is scriptural, methodical, efficient, practical, and realistic. In the midst of the systematic approach, the process to the desired change is spiritually enriching.

For years I have known and informed the author that her technical profession and corporate skill sets would be a wonderful gift in building the kingdom of God. It makes me proud to endorse and recommend someone who is a much needed gift to music ministry and even to church growth. I introduce to some and present to others music ministry consultant, music coach, professor, and now book author, Dr. Antonia Arnold-McFarland!

Best regards and blessings,
Pastor William Becton, Master of Theology, Life Christian University
William Becton Ministries, House of Worship, Charlotte, NC
Producer, Composer, Becthoveen Enterprises
Two-time Stellar Award Winner, International Charting Artist
Four Album Discography, Hit Single "Be Encouraged"

PREFACE

Early Years

I remember at the age of four enjoying watching my mother play the piano as she taught students played and sang popular songs after dinner. Watching me while she taught my older sister, Sonya, my mother soon noticed that I had music talent of my own. She initially did not think I was old enough for lessons but began teaching me to read music even before I learned to read words. She recognized my natural ability to play by ear and sought to nurture that. At age five, I realized I loved being a part of music ministry. I was already singing in the sunbeam choir and gained an early appreciation of corporate worship. My debut at piano was at Silver Hill United Methodist Church in Spartanburg, South Carolina. Despite my extreme nervousness, I played "Jesus Loves Me" on the piano while my mother, the music director, accompanied me on the organ. This moment was a turning point in my life that continues to manifest itself in me today in different facets.

Music Training

My formal music training began with piano lessons from my mother from ages four to six. Then she sent me to Yamaha School of Music until I was eight. From ages nine to 17, I studied classical piano at Converse Pre-College Music Department in Spartanburg. This was paralleled with eight years as a violinist in the School District 7 orchestra from fifth to twelfth grade. My college years included five years in New Horizons Choir at North Carolina State University, where I received weekly vocal enhancement and training on black sacred music. This has been an essential component of my professional music ministry abilities. During and after my doctoral studies, I received several sequences of mastery vocal training courses from Rozlyn Sorrell of Vocal Precision Studio in Raleigh, North Carolina. My musicianship and ministry knowledge continue to be shaped by music ministry colleagues, scholars, and mentors, including Pastor William Becton and Professor L. Stanley Davis.

Passion Meets Profession

My 25 years of experience in church music ministry is the foundation of my calling as a music ministry consultant and strategist. I have served in the capacity of staff musician, choir director, praise and worship leader, and music director in African-American churches in the Raleigh area. As an aspiring gospel artist with my ensemble Blessed Union, The Group, and an accomplished church musician, my passion for music ministry has been nurtured by the opportunities afforded. I am passionate about worship and music ministry because it speaks to the heart and brings hope and healing, even when words cannot. This is demonstrated in Scripture on various occasions to be the impetus for triumph and transformation. For example, in 1 Samuel 16:14–23, David played his harp well and relieved Saul of an evil spirit. In Acts 16:25–34, Paul and Silas prayed and sang hymns until an earthquake shook the foundation and chains off the prisoners. The Philippian jailer and his household were converted. My purpose is to lift up the name of the Lord, and He will draw all men unto Him (John 12:32). Therefore, it is not up to me to judge and reject souls. If worship is effective, people will be drawn unto Him in search of a more abundant life. His presence will be their light in darkness. Then on their own, they will desire to change their lives because they now see the light of life, which is hope through the message of Christ. The faults and shortcomings that had bound them in darkness will no longer rule them.

My formal education consists of a minor degree in African-American Studies and a Bachelor of Science in Mechanical Engineering from North Carolina State University (Raleigh, North Carolina), a Master of Business Administration from the University of Phoenix (Raleigh Campus/Online), and a Doctor of Ministry in Creative Arts from the Graduate Theological Foundation (Mishawaka, Indiana). I could not have imagined this combination of curriculums but now realize that this academic girding provides me with a hybrid mix of studies that influence my insight and lens for ministry. I am currently an adjunct professor in the Doctor of Ministry Program at Eastern Carolina Christian College and Seminary (Roanoke Rapids, North Carolina). This involvement with future scholars and peers in academia keeps me engaged and relevant in future possibilities for music ministry improvement. This exposure provides ongoing insights and connections.

It has not been a coincident that 25 years in music ministry has evolved alongside 20 plus years in a technical professional career. This has primarily been at John Deere, where I currently work as a Master Six Sigma Black Belt/Master Process Pro. As a certified Six Sigma Black Belt, I train and coach others on how to lead projects using Six Sigma Methodology and tools for problem resolution. This is an internationally recognized specialization that is applied in a variety of industries to enable quality and minimize defects. It is used to improve effectiveness, efficiency, business processes, and profitability. I see how it can be translated to improve music ministry and worship effectiveness.

My music experience and training, formal education, corporate experience, technical skills, and Six Sigma certification (in problem solving through project leading) uniquely position me to offer a niche perspective as a music ministry consultant. I believe God has allowed my passion for strategizing, problem solving, and music ministry to merge in order to discover new possibilities to improve worship effectiveness. I enjoy being able to creatively and innovatively apply these skills to music and arts ministry, a key ingredient to the corporate worship experience.

The Research Project

As a part of my doctoral research, I launched an initiative called Gospel Music One Sound Project to investigate the current-day landscape of gospel music in the local church, the community, and the music industry. My research included a symposium and concert headlining national gospel artist William Becton, whom I have understudied musically and spiritually since 2006. I plan to continue to package this research as seminars, webinars, books, and courses to help streamline the journey for those who are called to exalt, execute, employ, or lead worship from music (and arts) ministry to the music industry. My aim is to unify and renew the purpose of gospel music practitioners who labor in church, the community, and the gospel segment of the music industry.

The name *Gospel Music One Sound* was revealed to me as the measure of effectiveness in worship during my doctoral research and was inspired by reading 2 Chronicles 5:13. When the musicians and vocalists praised the Lord and gave Him thanks in unison as one sound, a thick cloud, which was the glory of the Lord, filled the temple. This is the goal for the ultimate Christian worship experience, with my specialty on the effectiveness of the African-American worship landscape.

Gospel Music One Sound Project is an ongoing effort that seeks best techniques to guide the church music ministry leader/worship leader/gospel artist. The gospel artist and church music ministry leader have an opportunity to work together and leverage the worship space comprised of the local church, community, and music industry marketplace, all for kingdom building.

ACKNOWLEDGMENTS

"For God so loved the world, that he gave his only begotten Son, that whosoever believeth in him should not perish, but have everlasting life" (John 3:16 KJV). For this reason, I must acknowledge God for all He has given me, all He has forgiven me of, and all He will grace me with in the future. He gave His son Jesus Christ so I could have fullness of life on earth and for eternity. My hope is that He will be pleased with the way I use the gifts and talents He has blessed me with.

Second, I acknowledge the musical influences in my family that planted seeds and continue to nurture my growth. This includes my parents, Raymond Arnold Jr. and the late Mary F. Arnold; my siblings, Dr. Sonya Arnold and Raymond (Trey) Arnold III; and my husband, Tony McFarland Sr. They are all musically inclined and have been a part of my musical being. Extended families from both my parents influenced me musically, especially in the church. My mother, my first piano teacher, played for the Ferguson Singers from Greenville, South Carolina. Her family includes a host of musicians and vocalists. My dad's mother, the late Maude Mathis, and her sister, Otis R. Miller, were pianists from the Rookard family of Spartanburg, South Carolina. They helped influence me musically in my early years of life.

Next I acknowledge my music colleagues who have been a part of my journey from Spartanburg to Raleigh, North Carolina, and current connections in other cities. These individuals make up the community of practitioners that have kept me inspired and engaged. This includes my piano teachers, orchestra conductors, community music groups, fellow church musicians and vocalists, vocal instructors, choir directors, church music directors, gospel choirs, pastors, mentors, music producers, and professors.

I thank my ambitious friends and confidants who are supportive, encouraging, and inspiring. These people are a part of my think tank and sounding board or merely a role model without even knowing it. They are not necessarily fellow musicians but people I have connected with along the milestones of life. Their endurance, achievements, and confidence in me motivate me to dream the impossible.

My interest in music ministry consulting was planted by the work of internationally respected musician, producer, author, and lecturer Steven Ford of sfordmusic.com. I have had the pleasure of meeting Mr. and Mrs. Ford and have leveraged his instructional style of work to improve music ministries I have worked with. I thank him for shaping and influencing me to join the ranks of laborers in this arena. He is considered an authority on music ministry in the African-American church and in the music industry.

I especially want to thank Ron Foreman, Eleania Ward, and the New Horizons Choir Alumni of North Carolina State University for my collegiate development in music ministry. I thank my colleagues of music ministry and music industry in the Raleigh-Durham, North Carolina, area for keeping me abreast of events to increase my skills, for being models of musicianship and artistry, and for affording me opportunities. In music ministry this includes Roland Perry II, Thomas Van Hook Jr., Norris Garner, Valerie Johnson, the late Doug Bynum, and other colleagues (past and present) in the Raleigh-Durham Triangle Chapter of the National Convention of Gospel Choirs and Chorus, Inc. In the music industry this includes Monroe and Marion Watson (Sound Audio Services), Marion and Justine Wiggins (Playground Studios), Alphonza Kee (Alphonza Kee Music/Consultant/Producer), James A. House (House Theatre Arts Group), James Stephen III (Comedian/Artist/Minister/JS3 Foundation), Dr. Mildred Summerville (Summerville Promotion and Production Company), and Reginald Graves (RJ Graves Productions).

My husband and I co-founded Blessed Union, The Group, in 2005. We share the same anniversary, as this group was birthed out of a collection of vocalists who sang at our wedding on May 22, 2005.

This also is the birthday of my mother, who planted the early seeds of music in me. It is not coincidental that these three "births" (my mother, my marriage, and my music) share this date. The full purpose is still yet to be revealed. I thank current members and alumni for being instrumental in my growth and entrusting me with their growth. Your participation has been invaluable and continues to be so. I am humbled when I realize the vast talent pool of past and present "generations" of the "BU" flavor. God has made room for each of your gifts. Bless you, Blessed Union, The Group, as your gifts bless others.

For over 10 years, my husband and I have been under the mentorship and spiritual and musical tutelage of Pastor William Becton. He is a wealth of knowledge and support for us spiritually and in our musical endeavors. He has poured into us and into our music ensemble, Blessed Union, The Group.

Thanks to Pastor K. Ray Hill (Maple Temple United Church of Christ, Raleigh, North Carolina), Pastor Kenneth Pugh (Hatcher Grove Baptist Church, Morrisville, North Carolina), Rev. Dr. William T. Newkirk (Oak City Baptist Church, Raleigh, North Carolina) and Pastor George Greene and First Lady Kerri West Greene (Christian Home Christian Church, Apex, North Carolina) for allowing me the opportunity to sharpen my gifts in your ministries at different times over the past 20 years and up to the present. I am grateful for being able to learn, contribute, and practice within your ministries. I drew so much from that toward writing this book.

Currently I attend World Overcomers Christian Church in Durham, North Carolina, under the leadership of Pastor Andy Thompson. I am thankful for the sound teaching and high standard of worship demonstrated by the music and worship arts ministry and the audio and media team. This collective effort sets the atmosphere for transformation and operates with a participatory worship model. This worship experience feeds my spirit as a worshiper. The Word enriches my daily Christian walk and insight as I seek balanced victory for the God-designed life.

This book is a by-product of Gospel Music One Sound Project, an initiative that launched as a result of my doctoral research on the evolution of African-American worship. Writing it would not have been possible without the expertise, knowledge, and support of these key individuals, organizations, and events:

Professor L. Stanley Davis (Black Sacred Music Historian, Scholar, and Clinician, Chicago, IL)

Dr. Raymond Wise (Gospel Music Scholar, Indiana University, Bloomington, IN)

Pastor William Becton (Gospel Artist and Pastor, House of Worship, Charlotte, NC)

Dr. C. Anthony Hunt (Project Advisor, Baltimore, MD)

Rev. Dr. William T. Newkirk (Senior Pastor, Oak City Baptist Church, Raleigh, NC)

Rev. Dr. Jean Brown (Ministerial Staff, Oak City Baptist Church, Raleigh, NC)

Mr. Richard Jones (Jones Printing Services, Raleigh, NC)

Dr. Dorothy Burns (Professor, Hampton University, Hampton, VA, and Baltimore, MD)

Rev. Dr. Haywood T. Gray (General Baptist State Convention of North Carolina, Raleigh, NC)

Ms. Rozlyn Sorrell (Vocal Extraordinaire, Vocal Precision Studios, Raleigh, NC)

Mr. Willie Hill (Inspire Productions of Kompass Studios, Raleigh, NC)

Mr. Donald "DJ" Freeman Jr (Choir Director, Deliverance Cathedral of Love, Raleigh, NC)

The organizations that have supported this journey include Graduate Theological Foundation (Mishawaka, Indiana), Oak City Baptist Church (Raleigh, North Carolina), Eastern Carolina Christian College and Seminary (Roanoke Rapids, North Carolina), Gospel Music One Sound Project participants, *Moving Forward and Facing the Future* 2016 Lecture attendees and support staff (John Riddick and Tabatha Archibald), The General Baptist State Convention of North Carolina (Rev. Dr. Haywood T. Gray), and the support of Christian Editing Services.

Tony and Toni (Arnold) McFarland
Thanks to you all for your support!

INTRODUCTION

What This Book Covers

This book focuses on the unique challenges and factors of the music and worship ministry of the African-American worship experience; however, the scriptures, tools, and processes transcend culture and ethnicity. The book is a product of the Gospel Music One Sound Project, an ongoing initiative seeking to renew purpose and improve effectiveness of the African-American worship experience in three venues: the church, the community, and the music industry.

Many churches still operate only in the frame of music ministry yet need to move forward with the perspective of music and worship arts ministry. They are not realizing this shift in worship culture across all ethnicities that positions them for growth. The skill set of personnel in the music and worship arts realm has grown beyond purely music. It is also important to note that music ministry and worship leaders are often music artists and in the frame of this book, gospel artists in the community pursuing the gospel music industry. There is a growing need for the church to understand the frame of ministry and industry and the set of procedures this brings. National, regional, and local gospel artists are a part of the landscape of worship. Some churches are producing their own artists and music. This changes the dynamics of skill sets, planning, budgeting, and operating the music and arts ministry.

The music and worship ministry plays a vital role in corporate worship. Advance planning and ongoing development is critical to ensure spiritual nourishment and effectiveness of all participants. This book discusses the practical and strategic steps to help the music and worship arts ministry learn from our past, realize our present state, and plan for the future. The Black Church offers a rich heritage in sacred music that requires special attention as it evolves to modern worship practices.

Why This Book Is Important to Churches and Ministry Leaders Today

Church and ministry leaders today are faced with the challenge of relevancy to the changing culture and advances around them. The aim is to sustain and grow the church with limited resources while meeting the needs of the congregation. The music and arts ministry is vital to the life of the church. It is important that leaders stay knowledgeable of the dynamics that affect them and that they regularly review their current position and strategy toward the vision.

How to Use This Book

This book is intended to be a practical and quick reference guide for music ministry leaders, musicians, worship leaders, and others who are responsible for growth in music and worship arts ministry. It is written primarily for use in the African-American worship experience in the local church, yet it can be applied to sacred music entities in the community and in pursuit of the music industry. Although the research is centered on the Black Church, solutions and tools are applicable multi-ethnically. The book is a supplement to the content provided in seminars, webinars, and advice based on my practical and professional experience in music and worship arts ministry. I apply my technical experience gained in Six Sigma, quality, project management, and coaching to help music ministries understand how to get from where they are currently to where they need to be in the future. My aim is to help ministries diagnose their gaps, constraints, and limitations in this area. This is done to help them implement practical solutions and to devise a strategy for long-term growth. We must first understand our past and where we are today in relation to the past. Next, we must understand our purpose and how it drives our calling for the future. Use this book as a step-by-step guide to success via the hybrid approach I have outlined. This study is most effective when used under my facilitation and guidance through the journey of transformation from the present to the future. It includes sample tools, quick reference charts, and visual aids to enhance understanding and to transfer knowledge.

Background Information

The content was first presented as a lecture on November 1, 2016, at the General Baptist State Convention of North Carolina. It is an excerpt of content compiled as a part of Gospel Music One Sound Project, which took place in November 2015. It focused on the evolving African-American worship experience in the local church, the community, and the gospel music industry. The issues were identified from two surveys (25–30 participants each), a panel discussion, and webinars that occurred as a part of the research. The primary demographic of participants included attendees of African-American churches in the Raleigh-Durham area that had an average weekly attendance of 300 or less (medium to small churches) who had leadership responsibilities in the music ministry or church. Their music ministries consisted of a youth choir, male choir, and an adult mix voice gospel choir and/or praise and worship leaders.

Gospel Music One Sound Project

Gospel Music One Sound Project is an ongoing initiative that was realized during the field experience and research intervention of my doctoral work. My Doctor of Ministry in Creative Arts was earned at The Graduate Theological Foundation in Mishawaka, Indiana. The title of my doctoral project is as follows:

THE EVOLUTION OF AFRICAN-AMERICAN WORSHIP: FROM MUSIC MINISTRY TO MUSIC INDUSTRY, AS PURSUED BY THE INDEPENDENT GOSPEL ARTIST FROM THE THOMAS DORSEY TO KIRK FRANKLIN ERA

The Biblical Foundation of Gospel Music One Sound Project is based on the following scripture:

> Indeed it came to pass, when the trumpeters and singers *were* as one, **to make one sound** to be heard in praising and thanking the LORD, and when they lifted up their voice with the trumpets and cymbals and instruments of music, and praised the LORD, *saying: "For He is* good, For His mercy *endures* forever," that the house, the house of the LORD, was filled with a cloud, so that the priests could not continue ministering because of the cloud; for the glory of the LORD filled the house of God.
>
> 2 Chronicles 5:13–14 [emphasis added]

Services Offered

My music ministry advising and consulting offer practical and strategic solutions to address issues in the music/worship ministry. I can be reached at LinkedIn (searched as *Antonia Arnold-McFarland*) or email eflatmajor@bellsouth.net for details.

CHAPTER ONE

Worship: Purpose, Foundation, and Application

My Position on the Topic of Worship

My doctoral research dives into an in-depth look at worship, defining it from a spiritual, secular, biblical, theological, and African-American cultural perspective. Despite this, I still have room for more research, study, growth, and understanding of worship. I consider myself a practitioner of worship with expert knowledge on the application of music and arts in ministry for the benefit of the corporate worship experience. My cultural experience is based on the African-American church, yet some aspects of my findings and teachings could be replicated across ethnicities.

Our Worship Space

From a practical sense, those who work in ministry need ongoing engagement in the topic of worship so the worship space where we labor stays relevant and effective for the evolving world we live in. As Christians, our worship space includes the community where we live, external influences from popular culture (music industry, television, radio, media, and Internet), and the local church. This book focuses on the worship space as music, the community, and the local church—the primary venue.

What Is Worship?

It is vital to understand clearly what worship is and what it is not. This understanding is important for leveling our knowledge before diving deeper.

Interactive Learning Activity:

In this chapter, you will see leading questions followed by an explanatory paragraph. Before reading past each question, in your own words, write down your thoughts in response to the leading question. Once you have done so, continue reading, comparing your answer with what is explained in that section. After you've read the explanation, pause and ask yourself, "What is the difference between what I just read and what I wrote as my answer to the leading question? Was I accurate? If not, why not? What will I do differently because of this awareness?"

The Basic Linguistic Definition of Worship

Merriam Webster Online Dictionary (*worship*, 2015) defines worship from a spiritual view (not necessarily Christian) and from a secular view. These definitions represent what society views as worship in the English language.

1) Reverence offered a divine being or supernatural power; an act of expressing such reverence; a form of religious practice with its creed and ritual
2) Extravagant respect or admiration for or devotion to an object of esteem; synonymous to idolatry

What Is the Purpose of Worship?

As Christians, the purpose of worship is to keep us spiritually fit to recalibrate us and redeem us back to Christ, allowing us to have a more fulfilling experience with God. We worship because we believe there are earthly and eternal benefits for redeeming our lives. This is evident in our mental and physical health, our finances, our marriage, our children, the friends we choose, our morals, and all that gives us a more abundant life. Our worship helps us reach what once seemed impossible. The local church, where we assemble as Christians for worship service and are involved in activities for spiritual growth, is our spiritual "fitness center." It's the "gym" where we work out regularly to exercise our "spiritual muscles" for the endurance (our faith) needed to overcome hurdles and obstacles as we run the marathon of life. The way we respond and behave outside the facilitated worship service as we interact with others in church, at work, or in the community is the real indicator of our spiritual strength and fitness.

What Makes Up the Foundation of Worship?

From a theological standpoint, worship is the foundation of our spiritual development in Christianity. There are two perspectives to keep in mind when studying worship: 1) the individual worship by each of us and 2) the collective or corporate worship of Christians.

What Does Our Individual Worship Look Like?

For the individual, worship is bowing down in submission to God because of our reverence. We express our worship by praying, singing, shouting, or dancing before the Lord. Our reverence precedes these acts of expression and should be demonstrated by our lifestyle. It is important for music and worship arts ministry participants to know this. These individuals need awareness of worship as a lifestyle. Their worshiper hearts reflect outwardly in their attitude and are demonstrated by their acts of expression.

I summarize these acts of expression by what I call the "M's" of worship: by mouth, by music, by motion, by motifs, and now by media. Worship Pastor Russell Henderson (2009) of IGNITE Worship Ministries categorizes expression of worship as by voice, posture, and hands. For example, *by voice* it is spoken, sung, and shouted. *By posture* includes bowing, standing, and dancing. *By hands* involves playing an instrument, clapping, and lifting of hands. The Bible offers examples of all these.

Outward and inward expressions result from authentic encounters with God. The anointing and spirit of the Lord is present when we find ourselves saying and doing things not controlled by our own will and motives. Our motivation is to please God and not man, surrendering to the will of God by our own desire and love for God. Worship is not an oppressive surrender. It is a welcomed surrender for our own benefit.

Worship is an overall lifestyle and is not limited only to what happens at church or other specific places or times. Leaders of worship and arts ministries must instruct on worship from the foundational approach and not just teach how it is expressed in service through singing, dance, media production, prayer, lifting up of hands, or shouting unto the Lord. My research, especially the work of Harold Best, helped me realize that we are all worshipers, whether we realize it or not. Non-believers are worshipers. At all times, we are either worshipping God or giving in and submitting to something else. The other choices could be our own will or the will of another person, object, thing, force, or thought to which we have submitted. There is risk in having free will to choose the direction of our worship. This can be detrimental to our well-being and soul, based on what or whom we choose to empower in our lives. Howard Best, a systematic theologian, explains this well in *Unceasing Worship, a Biblical Perspective on Worship and the Arts.* His book is a part of the literature review in my doctoral work. I recommend it for further study on worship (Best, 2003).

What Is Worship From a Biblical Perspective?

From a biblical standpoint, your lifestyle should demonstrate that you are applying the Word of God to your life. Your worship is your decision to live sacrificially, meaning you sacrifice your own desires for the benefit you will gain from choosing the will of God. We must study God's Word and receive sound teaching to learn His will for us. The effectiveness of worship is measured by the demonstrated Christ-like transformation of our mind-set and spirituality. Our goal is to have all aspects of our being in line with the teachings of Christ, not the will of our flesh or the world around us. Therefore, we must bow down to God and submit to Him as the authority over our lives.

This book focuses on music and artistic expressions of worship, but we must realize acts of worship are demonstrated in the Bible purely out of reverence, submission, and obedience to God, even when the worshipers found it uncomfortable, unpopular, or even painful. Christian Arts Pastor and Lead Worshiper Tom Curely (2012) reminds us of some of these expressions at WorshipTeamCoach.com. Abraham was willing to sacrifice Isaac in obedience to God, yet God provided a ram in the bush and Isaac was not sacrificed in Genesis 22: 9–13. The woman with the alabaster box sacrificed her expensive perfume by pouring it on Jesus's feet in Luke 7:37–38. She bowed at his feet as she washed them with her tears and wiped them with her hair. The greatest sacrifice of all was made when Jesus accepted his fate to die on the cross for our sins, out of his love for us and his obedience to God as told in Luke 22:41–43.

Following are a few Bible verses that speak to the foundation and essence of worship. They further explain the biblical expectation of true worshipers.

Here is a physical demonstration of the posture that expresses our heart: "Oh come, let us worship and bow down; Let us kneel before the Lord our Maker. For He *is* our God, and we *are* the people of His pasture, and the sheep of His hand" (Psalm 95:6–7).

Here is an explanation of what is expected spiritually. We are to worship God being led by His spirit and by the truth. We learn this from the gospel of Christ, the Word of God, and Jesus, the truth the way and the life (John 14:6). The following scripture further demonstrates this truth:

> "But the hour is coming, and now is, when the true worshipers will worship the Father in spirit and truth; for the Father is seeking such to worship Him. God *is* Spirit, and those who worship Him must worship in spirit and truth." (John 4:23–24)

Here is an explanation of what to be cautious of in our worship. It also explains what worship is not. Worship must be in the heart and not just on our lips. Worship must not be based merely on traditions and rules taught by man. These may not be the truth. The NIV version explains this in a way that cuts to the chase: "The Lord says: 'These people come near to me with their mouth and honor me with their lips, but their hearts are far from me. Their worship of me is based on merely human rules they have been taught'" (Isaiah 29:13).

Worship is demonstrated sacrificially. We give up the desires of our heart and of our flesh in order to worship Him in spirit and in truth. "I beseech you therefore, brethren, by the mercies of God, that you present your bodies a living sacrifice, holy, acceptable to God, *which is* your reasonable service" (Romans 12:1).

What Is Corporate Worship?

Corporate worship is the mandated assembly of Christians:

> And let us consider one another in order to stir up love and good works, not forsaking the assembling of ourselves together, as *is* the manner of some, but exhorting *one another,* and so much the more as you see the Day approaching. (Hebrews 10:24–25)

To understand corporate worship, I studied the work of Robert E. Webber (1996), a theologian on worship and the early church, who founded the Institute of Worship Studies. He realized that music ministry has evolved from only overseeing music and worship to a pastoral ministry that includes worship teaching, worship evangelism, worship spirituality, and counseling. Webber's focus on worship provides the corporate worship perspective and the role of music in aiding believers to experience God. This examination of music in worship exemplified in the Bible assists in developing the theological frame work. Robert E. Webber's *Complete Library of Christian Worship (A Brief History of Music in Worship)* provides a synopsis of music in the worship of the Old and New Testaments.

Webber notes that Jewish synagogue worship in the Old Testament and modern Christian services are similar in content and spirit, and music in both instances has been inseparable from worship. Psalms represent early heritage worship songs and periods of ancient Jewish culture. Synagogue music had cantors or soloists who were possibly trained in the temple Levitical ministry. There was also some congregation involvement.

Moses and his sister, the prophetess Miriam, are accredited with the first musical reference in the Bible. They sang thanksgiving when God delivered the Israelites from the Egyptians. Miriam played a tambourine and sang, "I will sing to the Lord, for he is highly exalted. Both horse and driver he has hurled into the sea" (Exodus 15:1 NIV).

As she sang and danced, other ladies followed. This expression of praise is one example of many in the Old Testament, especially in the book of Psalms.

Webber refers to two musical traditions in the Old Testament mentioned by Erik Routley. The first is *spontaneous and ecstatic* (found in scriptures below) and the second is *formal and professional.*

First Samuel 10:5–6 describes the time when Saul was preparing to become king of Israel and the prophet Samuel was providing instruction:

> After that you shall come to the hill of God where the Philistine garrison *is.* And it will hap-

> pen, when you have come there to the city, that you will meet a group of prophets coming down from the high place with a stringed instrument, a tambourine, a flute, and a harp before them; and they will be prophesying. Then the Spirit of the LORD will come upon you, and you will prophesy with them and be turned into another man.

Second Kings 3:15–16 describes the time when prophet Elisha foretold God's judgment. Music assisted in the worshiper's experience of God: "'But now bring me a musician.' Then it happened, when the musician played, that the hand of the LORD came upon him. And he said, 'Thus says the LORD': "Make this valley full of ditches."'"

Examples of the formal and professional exhibit of music in worship in the Old Testament are found in the book of Psalms and in 1 Chronicles as the ark of God was being moved to Jerusalem. These examples of music in the temple were initiated by King David, well known for his skillful music abilities as a harpist and hymn composer.

> Then David spoke to the leaders of the Levites to appoint their brethren *to be* the singers accompanied by instruments of music, stringed instruments, harps, and cymbals, by raising the voice with resounding joy. . . . Kenaniah, leader of the Levites, was instructor *in charge of* the music, because he *was* skillful. . . . David was clothed with a robe of fine linen, as were all the Levites who bore the ark, the singers, and Ch28enaniah the music master *with* the singers. David also wore a linen ephod. Thus all Israel brought up the ark of the covenant of the LORD with shouting and with the sound of the horn, with trumpets and with cymbals, making music with stringed instruments and harps. (1 Chronicles 15:16–17, 22, 27–28)

Psalm 150 displays the musical instrumentation found in ancient Hebrew worship. Webber notes that in ancient Hebrew worship the words of Scripture were never to be spoken without melody. Doing so would be considered inappropriate. Scripture was always sung in fervent cantillation and accompanied by instruments, which embellished the vocal melody. Psalm 150 shows an example of how dance was included in ancient Hebrew worship. This is a well-known Scripture reference in African-American worship as it demonstrates the celebrative praise akin to African-American heritage.

> Praise the LORD! Praise God in His sanctuary; Praise Him in His mighty firmament! Praise Him for His mighty acts; Praise Him according to His excellent greatness! Praise Him with the sound of the trumpet; Praise Him with the lute and harp! Praise Him with the timbrel and dance; Praise Him with stringed instruments and flutes! Praise Him with loud cymbals; Praise Him with clashing cymbals! Let everything that has breath praise the LORD. Praise the LORD! (Psalm 150)

An example of how unified singing and instrumentation in the formal and professional setting is significant in experiencing God in worship is found at the dedication of Solomon's temple. In the following passage, God was so pleased, he revealed his presence through the musical performance.

> And it came to pass when the priests came out of the *Most* Holy *Place* (for all the priests who *were* present had sanctified themselves, without keeping to their divisions), and the Levites *who were* the singers, all those of Asaph and Heman and Jeduthun, with their sons and their brethren, stood at the east end of the altar, clothed in white linen, having cymbals, stringed instruments and harps, and with them one hun-

> dred and twenty priests sounding with trumpets—indeed it came to pass, when the trumpeters and singers *were* as one, to make one sound to be heard in praising and thanking the LORD, and when they lifted up their voice with the trumpets and cymbals and instruments of music, and praised the LORD, *saying:*
>
> "*For He is* good, For His mercy *endures* forever," that the house, the house of the LORD, was filled with a cloud, so that the priests could not continue ministering because of the cloud; for the glory of the LORD filled the house of God. (2 Chronicles 5:11–15)

Music is not mentioned as extensively in the New Testament as in the Old Testament. As Webber points out in his assessment of the music in the New Testament from the worship library, most of the references are conceptual rather than literal. The instructions for music are found mainly in the epistles, most of them given by Paul. A demonstration of music as a tool for worship in the New Testament is found in Paul's instructions in the following passage (Webber, 1996).

> Therefore let him who speaks in a tongue pray that he may interpret. For if I pray in a tongue, my spirit prays, but my understanding is unfruitful. 15 What is *the conclusion* then? I will pray with the spirit, and I will also pray with the understanding. I will sing with the spirit, and I will also sing with the understanding. How is it then, brethren? Whenever you come together, each of you has a psalm, has a teaching, has a tongue, has a revelation, (and) has an interpretation. Let all things be done for edification. (1 Corinthians 14:13–15, 26)

Webber explains that Paul is calling for a balance between ecstasy and discipline in music making (as well as in praying) by asking that singing be done with the mind (or understanding) as well as in the spirit. He advises that singing (as well as teaching, revelations, and speaking in tongues) be done for edification along with all things. Following are some of the well-known passages instructing how music is to be executed among believers.

> Speaking to one another in psalms and hymns and spiritual songs, singing and making melody in your heart to the Lord. (Ephesians 5:19)

> Let the word of Christ dwell in you richly in all wisdom, teaching and admonishing one another in psalms and hymns and spiritual songs, singing with grace in your hearts to the Lord. And whatever you do in word or deed, *do* all in the name of the Lord Jesus, giving thanks to God the Father through Him. (Colossians 3:16–17)

Webber brings to light the fact that in the New Testament the use of music in worship was exceedingly broad. He states that what the New Testament leaves unsaid about music is a healthy quality. Webber undergirds this understanding in the following scripture: "I know and am convinced by the Lord Jesus that *there is* nothing unclean of itself; but to him who considers anything to be unclean, to him *it is* unclean" (Romans 14:14).

Webber states that the distinction therefore between the pagan concept of the empowerment of things and the Christian concept of discernment among things, none of which are impure or empowered in themselves, overrides any opinion that the early church set a standard in music that was rigid, unchangeable, and limited. Webber concludes that the range of musical practice in the New Testament is rather to be construed as broadly as possible because it is based on a principle that speaks to a total way of life, including music.

These concepts reviewed by Webber apply to my thesis research in several ways. As the literature review revealed, a dichotomy in African-American worship styles was unveiled in the early developments of African-American worship. This dichotomy set the boundaries for denominational styles; the ecstatic style was more favored by the Pentecostal congregations and the formal and professional style by the Protestant churches, influenced by European worship. The black sacred music that evolves from spirituals to gospel music flows more closely with the ecstatic style. His assessment of the New Testament's philosophy of musical practices as a part of the total way of life can be viewed as a liberating perspective on how gospel music should go beyond the four walls of the church. This includes going into untapped aspects of life such as television, radio, and leisure listening.

What Is African-American Worship?

In the context of this work, African-American worship is worship influenced by the social and cultural experiences of African-Americans. The focus of this work is on African-American Christian worship. The worship space goes beyond the four walls of the church. The gospel artist and others recognized as key figures in Christianity can be a part of mainstream popular culture on television, in movies, in print, in online media, and in the music and entertainment industry. This occurs at the risk of commercialization, which can dilute authenticity. According to African-American music and worship scholar Melva Wilson Consten (1993), the worship of African-American Christians is informed by at least four streams of tradition: traditional African primal world views; Judeo-Christian religion; African-American folk religion, which emanated from world views shaped in the American context in a crisis of slavery and oppression; and Western/Euro-American Christianity. She further explains African-American leitourgia (liturgy) as the work of the people in ritual action, ministry, and service. It is reflective of the experiences of a particular people deeply aware of the power and promise of God.

The definition of African-American worship is further synthesized in my doctoral work (Arnold-McFarland A. M., 2016).

The African-American worship experience is ever evolving. Taking note of the full worship space (music industry, community, and church) is necessary for churches to be effective in growing in ways that address the needs of the African-American community. My research explored the topic of gospel music ministry versus the music industry. In the African-American church, there is an ongoing debate on what is considered acceptable for worship service and the responsibility of the gospel artist to represent ministry over industry. The driving force and motivation of the argument is centered on one's perception of worship. There are differences in opinion of what qualifies as true and authentic worship, which is the key ingredient in music ministry.

When popular culture influences the practices in the church, especially in music and worship arts, Christians often lean to the following scripture for theological support to avoid appearing like the world: "And do not be conformed to this world, but be transformed by the renewing of your mind, that you may prove what *is* that good and acceptable and perfect will of God" (Romans 12:2).

This conflict of interest faced by the gospel artist brings into question the motivation and authenticity of his or her worship of God. In other words, as Christians, adherence or conformance to His perfect will, which is defined by the Word of God, is a measure of how well we worship Him. The decisions we set our minds to should be acceptable in His eyes and not conform to the world. Now that we have defined worship and have a multi-faceted understanding of worship, we can examine the conformance of the demonstration of worship by the gospel artist to the theology of worship in the Holy Bible.

What Is Expected of Those Called to the Music and Worship Arts Ministry?

Those who feel they are called to participate or lead in the music and worship arts ministry, either in the local church or as a gospel artist in the music industry, should be aware of the applicable instructions in Scripture. These explain what is required and what is ideal for their skills to be used to help others experience God through song, dance, visual media, and the fine arts. My challenge to modern-day Levites is to compile a list of all the scriptures in Bible that refer to music and worship arts. Those called to this vital ministry should seek to model their worship and technical ability after the skills of the Levites in the First and Second Books of Chronicles.

As mentioned earlier, in 1 Chronicles 15:16 David spoke to the leaders of the Levites to appoint their brethren *as* singers to raise their voices with resounding joy, accompanied by instruments of music, stringed instruments, harps, and cymbals. In 1 Chronicles 15:22 Chenaniah was in charge of singing based on his skill. In 1 Chronicles 25:7 Levites were all trained and skilled in music of the Lord.

It is important to note that the Levites were appointed based on their anointing and skill. They were not volunteers. Leaning to volunteer participation causes a foundational flaw and ongoing challenges in music ministries today. All participants are not spiritually and technically ready.

Participants' lifestyle of worship should give them a heart of servitude and humility. This is discussed in detail in Steven Ford's *In Your Music Department Ministry or Misery* (2009). This book is a great resource for enhancing the gifts of music ministry. It is one I have used for hands-on improvements after a strategy and plan have been devised for a music ministry.

Summary

The topic of worship is broad and complex because of the various perceptions of what worship means. It deserves ongoing study and continuous discussion in the local church. I've realized that as a result of misalignments and limited understanding of what worship is, the capacity for effectiveness of worship is also limited. The worship will only be as effective as the understanding and unity of those leading the worship. It will also be only as effective as the understanding of the individual who is worshipping. This in turn creates a limited view of people's abilities and perception of their own abundant life.

As stated earlier, the ultimate worship experience and standard of measure for corporate worship is found in 2 Chronicles 5:11–14. God was so pleased with the worship, He revealed his presence through the musical performance. To reach this level, participants must demonstrate authentic worship, nurtured by their lifestyle and regular practice of worship. This scripture is the key teaching that gave way to the name of my initiative Gospel Music One Sound Project. The trumpeters and singers (who represent the worship artists) were as one, making one sound to be heard in praising and thanking the Lord. We must be in one accord spiritually as we lead others to experience God in worship. This will result in one sound. This is the charge to all worship artists in our worship platforms (the local church, the music industry, and the community).

Understanding worship is vital to the life of the church and to the body of Christ. It is vital for obtaining effectiveness in the worship and arts ministry. Writing this chapter was a struggle because it was hard to scope down the discussion to the elements specific only to improving music ministry. My belief is that to be most effective, people must see the whole picture before understanding how they can contribute individually to the whole. This section is lengthy, but as the author, truncating this topic convicted me and made me feel as though I was taking a risky shortcut or entrusting someone's life decisions to a "cliff note" understanding of the Bible. My desire is to do my best to well equip people spiritually who are involved in key roles that affect the spirituality of others. The remaining chapters of this book include further discussion of equipping ministry leaders in music and arts, so they can address emerging issues and challenges.

References

Arnold-McFarland, A. M. (2016). *The evolution of African-American worship: from music ministry to music industry, as pursued by the independent gospel artist, from the Thomas Dorsey to the Kirk Frankline Era*. Raleigh, NC: Eflat Major Publishing. Retrieved from https://issuu.com/eflatmajorpublishing/docs/research_project_-_dmin_-_creative_

Best, H. (2003). *Unceasing worship, a biblical perspective on worship and theater arts*. Downers Grove: Intervarsity Press.

Costen, M. (1993). *African-American Christian worship*. Nashville: Abingdon Press.

Curely, T. (2012). *The five greatest expressions of worship in The Bible. WorshipTeamCoach.com*. Retrieved from https://www.worship-teamcoach.com/blog/2012/08/31/the-5-greatest-expressions-of-worship-in-the-bible

Ford, S. (2009). *Is your music department ministry or misery?* Middletown: S. Ford Music Publishing.

Henderson, R. (2009). Nine expressions of worship. *ChurchLeaders.com*. Retrieved from https://churchleaders.com/worship/worship-how-tos/138587-nine-expressions-of-worship-david-s-lead.html

Webber, R. E. (1996). *A brief history of music in worship*. The Complete Library of Christian Worship. *WorshipLibrary.com*. Retrieved from https://www.worshiplibrary.com/library/music-and-the-arts-in-christian-worship/music-in-worship/a-brief-history-of-music-in-worship/

"Worship." (2015). *Merriam-Webster*. Retrieved from https://www.merriam-webster.com/dictionary/worship

CHAPTER TWO

The Black Church and Music: How Did We Get Here? A Look at the Past That Has Shaped Our Present

The African-American worship experience is unique in that it has been influenced by an array of social, political, and economic challenges faced by African-Americans. In my quest to understand the evolution of this worship experience, I had to parallel my research with a historical trace of African-Americans, starting with the arrival of enslaved Africans to Jamestown, Virginia, in 1619 and other events up to 2015. This book includes noted evolutions up to 2017. Before we dive into the African-American worship experience, let's summarize and level our knowledge on terminology referenced in my research and in this book (Arnold-McFarland A. M., 2016).

What Is a Gospel Artist?

A gospel artist is a soloist, choir, or group that performs gospel music (as described in the definition) in pursuit of a sustainable ministry and business position in the gospel music industry.

What Is the Gospel Music Industry?

The gospel music industry is a segment of the larger music industry. It is a segment of the Christian music industry that focuses on commercial level production, distribution, and sales of music and related products, services, events, and performances. My research focuses on gospel music that appeals to African-American culture.

What Are the Main Platforms for African-American Worship?

The main platforms for African-American worship are better comprehended after first understanding what *worship* is (see chapter 1 for further detail). As defined by *Merriam-Webster Online Dictionary* ("worship," 2015), *worship* is reverence offered a divine being or supernatural power; *also:* an act of expressing such reverence. In the context of this work, African-American worship is worship that is influenced by the social and cultural experiences of African-Americans.

This work focuses on African-American Christian worship. Worship space goes beyond the four walls of the church. Three venues or platforms examined in this discussion are the church, the community, and the music (and entertainment) industry. The gospel artist and others recognized as key figures in Christianity can be a part of mainstream popular culture on television, in movies, in print and online media, and in the music industry. These integrations occur at the risk of commercialization, which can dilute and compromise the authenticity of purpose.

What Is African-American Spirituality?

African-American spirituality emerged from the influence of African spirituality when enslaved Africans first came to North America in 1619 and were settled in Jamestown, Virginia. African-American spirituality is the foundation of the worship of African-Americans, the vast majority of them being Christians, who are the focus of this study. According to African-American music and worship scholar Melva Wilson Consten (1993), the worship of African-American Christians is influenced by at least four streams of tradition: traditional African primal world views; Judeo-Christian religion; African-American folk religion, which emanated from world views shaped in the American context in a crisis of slavery and oppression; and Western/Euro-American Christianity. She further explains African-American *leitourgia* (liturgy) as the work of the people through ritual action, ministry, and service. It is reflective of the experiences of a particular people deeply aware of the power and promise of God. The definition of African-American worship as an evolution from African spirituality is further synthesized in my doctoral research, yet for the sake of this book, we will review only the highlights.

The African primal world view was considered primitive and not acceptable to those who enslaved the Africans in America. The captives were forced to convert to the Western world's Europeanized Protestant Christianity. The forced conversion process lacked understanding and consideration of African spirituality. The African spirituality and primal world view saw no distinction between sacred and secular because one should always want to live in harmony with nature. All aspects of life already included reverence to a supreme being. Sacred and secular life were one and the same. The Western world religious lens could not digest this unfamiliar perspective on spirituality. It overlooked parallels between the primal view and Christianity such as the reverence to a supreme being, the concept of after life with ancestors, and the concept of prophesy and visions (Costen, 1993).

Were Enslaved Africans Already Exposed to Christianity?

Western slave masters and European missionaries alike ignored or failed to realize that history in the Bible that they "taught" to Africans took place in Africa and regions nearby. Some slaves were already Christians, yet with an African perspective. BBC World Service *Story of Africa* (2014) reports that the Christian communities of North Africa were among the earliest to exist in the world during the first and early second century AD. It further states that Christianity was brought from Jerusalem to Alexandria on the Egyptian coast in AD 60. It was brought by Mark, one of the four evangelists. This occurred possibly before or around the same time Christianity spread to Northern Europe. The BBC World Service further explains that Islam overtook the spread of Christianity in the seventh century, yet Christianity remained in pockets of North Africa and was the chosen religion of the Ethiopian Empire (2014). According to *God in America, The Black Church,* a documentary aired in 2013 by PBS, the first enslaved Africans from the kingdoms of Ndongo and Kongo in present-day Angola and the coastal Congo are believed to have been baptized Catholic. These kingdoms had been conquered in 1500 by the Portuguese, who brought Catholicism to West Africa at that time (Mellowes, 2010).

Yes, Christianity was in Africa before enslaved Africans were brought to America. In *Christianity Today* (2008) Elesha Coffman provides explanations and scriptural references in "What Does History Say About the First Christians in Africa?" She references Acts 8: 26–40 where Phillip met an Ethiopian eunuch who was reading the book of Isaiah. Phillip explained to him that the scripture he was reading was about Jesus being the sacrificial lamb for our sins. Phillip baptized the eunuch and continued evangelizing with the good news of Christ. For deeper study on this topic, Coffman's article refers the reader to visit online *Christianity Today Christian History* issue 51: Heresy in the Early Church, issue 64: Antony and the Desert Fathers, issue 67: Augustine, issue 79: The African Apostles, and *A History of Christianity in Africa* by Elizabeth Isichei (SPCK/Eerdmans, 1995).

What Is the Black Church?

A discussion on music of the African-American Church tradition and worship experience must begin with a foundational understanding of the Black Church (the African-American Church) and how important it is to African-Americans. It is important for current day practitioners of gospel music to understand the history of the Black Church, its denominations and belief systems, and its worship experience in the difference settings.

The term *the Black Church* must not be misinterpreted as a monolithic description of African-American Christianity. According to the PBS documentary *God in America, The Black Church* (Mellowes, 2010) this term evolved from the term *the Negro Church*, discussed in W.E.B. Dubois's pioneering research project on African-American Protestants. This academic study was completed at the turn of the twenty-first century and revealed the diversity and decentralization of the African-American Protestant faith. Scholars, including those of the documentary *God in America, The Black Church* and *The African-American Heritage Hymnal* (GIA Publications, Inc., 2001) have noted that the term *the Black Church* today includes the seven major historically black denominations with which 80% of black Christians are affiliated:

African Methodist Episcopal Church (A.M.E.)

African Methodist Episcopal Zion Church (A.M.E.Z.)

Christian Methodist Episcopal (C.M.E, formerly Colored Methodist Episcopal)

The National Baptist Convention, U.S.A., Incorporated (N.B.C)

The National Baptist Convention of America, Unincorporated (N.B.C.A.)

The Progressive National Baptist Convention (P.N.B.C.)

The Church of God in Christ (C.O.G.I.C.)

Today the term *the Black Church* is used generically to represent numerous denominational and non-denominational churches and Christians of African-American descent. The roots of the Black Church tradition grew out of a theology and faith forged by oppression and suffering from enslavement and segregation. The Black Church has provided empowerment and liberation from socio-economic strongholds and is still needed to inspire and lead the black community.

African-American worship has continued to evolve in such a way that the "Religious Portrait of African-Americans" in the *2007 Pew Religious Landscape Survey* revealed standout and distinctive statistics on African-American religious practices and beliefs. The study showed that 79% of African-Americans reported religion as very important in their lives, a higher statistic than the 56% of all U.S. adults with the same report.

Fifty nine percent (59%) of African-Americans belong to the historically black Protestant denominations (referred to as the Black Church), 15% to evangelical Protestant churches, 4% to mainline Protestant, 5% to Catholicism; 12% report as unaffiliated, 5% as *other* (includes Muslims, Jews, Buddhist, and Hindu), and 1% as unknown or refused to answer.

The study revealed that 70% of the unaffiliated African-Americans voiced absolute certainty that God exists. This is more than the 73% of affiliated mainline Protestant (US overall) and 70% of Catholics (US overall). The study noted that 88% of African-Americans overall have absolute certainty that God exists (The Pew Forum on Religion and Public Life, 2008).

The study also looked at religious practices such as frequency of prayer, attendance of service, and absolute certainty that God exists. The key takeaway from these measures is that African-Americans are considered the most religiously committed racial group in the nation.

In 2014, Pew Research Center provided the results of America's Changing Religious Landscape.

A comparison with the 2007 research reveals that Christianity across all main line traditions is on a decline, and the number of Christians unaffiliated to a traditional denomination is increasing.

The historically black Protestant tradition has sustained numbers and remained stable at approximately 15 million from 2007 to the 2014 survey.

David Briggs, a reputable voice on religious research and a Yale Divinity School graduate and writer for the Association of Religion Archives, published a blog article in the *Huffington Post* entitled (Are Black Americans the Most Religious and Virtuous of All?" As a white American and religious analyst, he provides a data-based view of African-American Christianity. The fact that he is a white American removes bias from his results (Briggs, 2015).

Briggs (2015) references several reputable research studies, including the *National Survey of American Life*, which revealed blacks as the most religious and the most virtuous demographic in the US, scoring higher than whites on seven of nine virtues. When compared with whites, blacks are more humble, more gracious to God, more compassionate to strangers, and more likely to provide emotional support and tangible help to strangers. Briggs's article, based on his research, states that many predominantly white churches are not making spiritual growth a priority. His article also notes that the Black Church is empowering and spiritually nurturing to attendees and that spirituality is at the core of the impact to community life, health, and economics.

He states that black churches are taking a leading role in economic empowerment. Briggs notes that 42% of black Protestants were encouraged to start a business, which is three times higher than evangelicals and mainline Protestants who received similar encouragement, per the 2010 Baylor Religious Survey. Blacks who are frequent church goers and active volunteers are less likely to feel overwhelmed by personal challenges. His article states that sociologist Gary Oats of Bowling Green State University notes the inoculative potential of the Black Church as a faith community (Briggs, 2015).

Briggs references the advocacy of sociologist Sandra Barnes of Vanderbilt University for more nuance research on the evolving role of religion in the lives of African-American and the relevance of the Black Church in contemporary America. She states that the Black Church has a lot to offer the larger religious landscape and the nation if "we," non-blacks, choose to pay attention. The Black Church faces challenges with membership retention of young adults in smaller churches as megachurch growth increases, yet the losses are more severe in white churches. The Black Church is still able to keep the faith in challenging times (Briggs, 2015).

Another current-day voice and authority on church growth is Dr. Ed Stetzer. He is a contributor to *Christianity Today* and a world-renowned church planter, pastoral trainer, the president of Lifeway Research, and the executive director of the Billy Graham Center for Evangelism. Stetzer, a white American, shared the insight of lessons to be learned from the Black Church based on an interview with his friend in ministry Pastor Charlie Dates, senior executive pastor of historically black Progressive Baptist Church in Chicago, Illinois. His article is a must-read called "We Can Learn from the Black Church When We Are Pushed to the Margins. "He claims that the gospel of Jesus Christ enables us to live in the world and to prosper therein without being loved by the world. The historical Black Church is a witness on how to do this. He writes that Christianity proper has been confused with the expansion of white cultural privilege. The day is approaching soon when American evangelicalism will learn what it feels like to live on the margins on of society (Stetzer & Dates, 2016).

This research and the statistics have brought visibility and attention to the strengths of the worship culture of the Black Church and the untapped resource it could be to mainline Protestant and evangelical churches. The survey results have intrigued theologians, scholars, and Christian worship experts to learn from the practices of the Black Church. There are still opportunities for improvement, yet the engaging worship culture characteristic of the Black Church is one of her strengths. Verbal participation and the spirit of celebration make the worship experience unique and empowering. These characteristics have been a part of the outward expressions of African worship that were suppressed and forbidden by the white slave master. What was once rejected is now accepted as spiritual strength.

Why Is This Information Important to the Evolution of African-American Worship?

These research results reveal a charge to the Black Church that goes beyond the black community. We hold the key to unlocking the spiritual growth of the nation because of the demonstration of our faith in our socio-economic journey in the US. We have the faith muscles to move mountains, and that is being recognized by non-black denominations. The effectiveness of African-American worship can have a significant impact on the faith growth of other ethnicities. It is important that we realize and recognize what has worked well in the Black Church. How will we use these results to move forward and face our future? We must realize and recognize what is not working well. Closing these gaps presents an opportunity to experience a more abundant and transformed life. This is pending effective execution and application of the Word of God and taking strategic action to position the church for growth. A key ingredient to bringing this transformation into reality is the effectiveness of our worship.

Why Should We Be Interested in Learning the History of the Black Church and the African-American Worship Experience?

It is important to have at least a basic understanding of the history of the African-American worship experience to fully realize the opportunity we have before us. We must look at the origins of African-American spirituality in America and understand how the social-economic struggles from enslavement and everything leading to and including present circumstances have shaped African-American worship. Understanding this journey also helps people individually identify with the influences that shaped their worship and spirituality. It helps people see the overall spiritual evolution that has shaped African-American worship and then realize their own spiritual formation.

My doctoral research leveraged the chronological gospel music timeline of Dr. Raymond Wise (2002) and scholarly tutelage under black sacred music historian Professor L. Stanley Davis (2015). The following historical graphic evolves from the information I compiled in 2015, based on my research of these two key scholars and on my prior findings. This graphic provides key factors of the spiritual music that evolved, shaped by the tribulations and triumphs in the lives of African-Americans. A key theme in the timeline is that controversy has been the forerunner of change spiritually, socially, and even musically for the church. Rejection and oppression, once in the forefront of black lives, still exist in the backdrop of history.

The chart does not include the artifacts, cultural norms, and indicators of engagement in African-American worship. These artifacts can occur whenever a few or more decide to celebrate God and "have church," as it is called by African-American Christians. Spiritual encounters transcend denominational differences and are even more evident in some. The black preachers "hoop" accompanied by a Hammond organ and soulful singing are characteristics of African-American worship. These elements are key ingredients that stir up the congregation. Testimonies, picturesque Bible stories, outbursts, shouts, dancing, and physical and verbal response from the congregation are cultural elements that have survived in African-American worship since its inception. These emotional responses and engagement prick the heart, and a transformational word from God pricks the soul.

The Historical Trace of the Evolution of Music Ministry in African-American Worship 1619–2017

African-American Historical Timeline and Topics in the Socio-Economic Climate	Black Sacred Music Era	Spiritual Art Form Produced by the Climate	Worship Space	Key Notes and Contributions
Pre-Emancipation (1619–1865) Africans in America first arrival at Jamestown, VA, in 1619 as captives in the institution of slavery American Revolutionary War (1775–1783)	Pre-Gospel and Pre-1900 Eras	Ditties, hollers and folk spirituals (Call and response with leader of group singing)	Plantation work fields (based on African religion practices), brush arbors, and harbors Some slaves attending church with slave masters but only allowed to sit in segregated places First African Baptist (1773), Savannah, GA Richard Allen establishes Bethel AME congregation (1794), Philadelphia, PA	Evolvement of native songs from Africa into field work songs. Once slaves forced into westernized Christianity, biblical text evolves into folk spirituals sung at secret meeting places and for code communication Talking drums eventually replaced by these coded songs

African-American Historical Timeline and Topics in the Socio-Economic Climate	Black Sacred Music Era	Spiritual Art Form Produced by the Climate	Worship Space	Key Notes and Contributions
Civil War (1861–1865) Reconstruction Era (1865–1877) and Post Emancipation up to 1900 Jim Crow Era starts and enacts legalized segregation in the South, post-Reconstruction	Pre-Gospel and Pre-1900 Eras	Folk spirituals evolve into Negro spirituals "Lined" hymns Devotional congregational singing, call and response, note singing led by spiritual leader	Early Black Churches grow; a spiritual dichotomy evolves. Baptist and Methodist conservatism vs. Holiness and Pentecostal spontaneity COGIC founded by Charles Mason (1895)	Fisk Jubilee Singers' introduction of concert anthem- style Negro spirituals in 1871 as they tour the world Some congregational singing without music
Educational Empowerment (1900–1920s) Beginning of First Great Migration North in response to WW I (1914–1918) and the Jim Crow Era	Pre-Gospel, Post-1900 Transitional Era	Improvised hymns (color, timbre, phrasing, melody, rhythm) Gospel hymns, Negro spirituals, anthems Note singing Devotional songs National Baptist Hymn Book (1906)	Mainline churches Morning worship service	Charles Tinsley and Lucie Campbell write gospel hymns Nathaniel Dett brings classical influence to black sacred music and establishes Hampton Institute School of Music; HBCU choirs tour, singing Negro Spirituals Lucie Campbell Music Director of the Baptist National Convention (1916) exposes the Baptist church to gospel hymns

African-American Historical Timeline and Topics in the Socio-Economic Climate	Black Sacred Music Era	Spiritual Art Form Produced by the Climate	Worship Space	Key Notes and Contributions
Harlem Renaissance (New Negro Movement) (1920s–1930s) The Great Depression (1929–1939) Beginning of Black Muslim Movement (1930s) Strides in athletics, education, fine arts, performing arts, and activism (1930s–1940s) Jim Crow segregation continues World War II (1939–1945)	Development (1920s–1930s) and Traditional Gospel Eras (1930–1945)	Gospel music genre; transition as premier black sacred music starts Jubilee quartet style Gospel songs Note singing	Mainline churches, afternoon concerts, and community programs Church conventions and conferences disseminate music	*Gospel Pearls* published (1921) Thomas Dorsey fuses gospel lyrics to blues progressions (1932). Gospel music industry's early seeds are planted. Field hollers/work songs beget blues/jazz Spirituals beget gospel Chicago the mecca for gospel music; Thomas Dorsey founds the National Convention of Gospel Choirs and Chorus, Inc. in Chicago (1932) Female soloists emerge; examples are Willie Mae Ford Smith, Roberta Martin, Sallie Martin Mahalia Jackson, and Roberta Thorpe Male quartet and harmony groups evolve; examples are the Foster Singers, Dixie Hummingbirds, and the Golden Gate Quartet All-female choirs/ ensembles emerge; Sallie Martin Singers, and the Ward Singers Martin and Morris Publishing established by Sallie Martin and composer Kenneth Morris

African-American Historical Timeline and Topics in the Socio-Economic Climate	**Black Sacred Music Era**	**Spiritual Art Form Produced by the Climate**	**Worship Space**	**Key Notes and Contributions**
Cold War with USSR starts (1947) Post-war economic boom does not benefit women and minorities Korean War (1950–1953) Vietnam War starts (1955) Growing racial tensions in America Civil Rights Era launches dynamic change, was against violent resistance at its start (1954–1968)	Golden Age of Gospel (1945–1960s)	Gospel music accepted in most black congregations by the 1940s Prior traditional styles included *The Free Will Baptist Hymnal (1958)*	Rejection of gospel music in the formative years by some black churches creates a new sustainable cultural space in the black community called the local gospel circuit Some gospel artists appear in secular venues (nightclubs, TV shows, etc.) Public protests activities	Soloist, quartet group, ensemble singing thrives; The Caravans peak in the 1950s Influence of quartet groups on the Motown look and sound Influence of gospel on rock and roll Dorsey, Lucie Campbell, Sallie Martin, and Roberta Martin arrange gospel hymns for choirs, ensembles, and soloists The congregation and audience become observers in worship; scholars call this a sociological consequence and a new homiletical gospel experience By the 1950s, the Gospel Highway connects artists across the nation Gospel music publication evolves. Artists get recording contracts and airplay and reach celebrity status.

African-American Historical Timeline and Topics in the Socio-Economic Climate	**Black Sacred Music Era**	**Spiritual Art Form Produced by the Climate**	**Worship Space**	**Key Notes and Contributions**
Civil Rights (1960s) Mid to later years—Malcom X, JFK, Bobby Kennedy, Dr. Martin Luther King, Medger Evers, and local heroes among the lives sacrificed	Golden Age overlaps with Modern Traditional Era (1960–1967)	Choir arrangements of gospel music Prior traditional styles continue	Mainline churches Community venues, choir concerts Conferences and conventions Local gospel circuit	Dr. Mattie Moss Clark revolutionizes gospel choir singing James Cleveland introduces choir recordings and new artists. Establishes GMWA to train musicians, singers, and artists Gospel and secular artists leverage their celebrity to influence the Civil Rights Movement The Staple Singers, Mahalia Jackson, and young Aretha Franklin a few from this Civil Rights Era Quartet and traditional groups gain popularity

African-American Historical Timeline and Topics in the Socio-Economic Climate	Black Sacred Music Era	Spiritual Art Form Produced by the Climate	Worship Space	Key Notes and Contributions
Close of Civil Rights Era (post King assassination) End of Vietnam War (1975) Operation Push and Rainbow Coalition merge (1971) Black Power Movement of the 1970s Alex Haley's *Roots* series airs on TV (1977) *Belmont Report of 1979* reveals the effects of the unrevealed 40-year Tuskegee syphilis study on black males without their consent	Overlaps modern contemporary (late 1960s–1970s)	Choir arrangements of gospel music Classical-influenced gospel music emerges from classically trained composers New *National Baptist Hymnal* (1977)	Mainline churches Community venues: choir concerts and academia Local gospel circuit Gospel music industry	Shirley Caesar's solo career underway Gospel music takes sustainable presence at HBCUs (1960s–1970s) and revolutionizes music departments Black sacred music ensembles emerge at pre-dominantly white colleges R&B, blues, jazz fusion with gospel is evident Edwin Hawkins release of "O Happy Day" (1969), which reaches #1 on the pop charts, coins him as the Father of Contemporary Gospel Andrea Crouch sparks multi-cultural interest, forerunning the Christian contemporary genre, coined the Father of Modern Gospel Music

African-American Historical Timeline and Topics in the Socio-Economic Climate	Black Sacred Music Era	Spiritual Art Form Produced by the Climate	Worship Space	Key Notes and Contributions
Liberty City riot against police brutality (1980); police acquitted, 11 killed MLK holiday established U.S. invasion of Granada (1983) Blacks make strides and milestones in politics, sports, entertainment, media, and science Vanessa Williams becomes first black Miss America First black astronaut in space: Guy Bluford (1983) Black Astronaut Ronald McNair dies with others in Challenger explosion (1986) HIV/AIDs crisis in the black community Lead poisoning in the black community identified Economic disparities in housing, jobs, healthcare, and education	Modern contemporary emerging trends (1980–1990)	Choir music flourishes *Songs of Zion* Hymnal has songs of heritage and tradition. Captures the contemporary black experience (1981) Urban culture influences gospel styles Fusions with rock, jazz, soul, and R&B become evident	Mainline churches Mega churches Word-based ministries Multicultural churches Community venues: choir concerts and academia Gospel music industry and touring circuit	Gospel music expands as a sustainable genre in black music Gospel record labels emerge James Cleveland starts King Records to provide artists with fair deals and flexibility Stellar Awards established. More gospel music industry celebrities emerge Mainstream artists include Shirley Caesar (Queen of Gospel), Milton Brunson and the Thompson Community Singers, the Winans, the Hawkins family, Andre Crouch, the Mississippi Mass Choir, Walt Whitman and the Soul Children of Chicago, Thomas Whitfield, Richard Smallwood, the Clark Singers, and Vanessa Bell Armstrong Gospel music gains nationally syndicated TV and radio shows Print media and magazines emerge. *Bobby Jones Gospel* launches on BET

African-American Historical Timeline and Topics in the Socio-Economic Climate	Black Sacred Music Era	Spiritual Art Form Produced by the Climate	Worship Space	Key Notes and Contributions
				Tours and concerts evolve in production level as demonstrated by the Andre Crouch, the Winans and Commissioned, and the Hawkins Family Secular artists include gospel roots on secular albums. "Jesus is Love" by Lionel Ritchie is a major hit John P. Kee and Hezekiah Walker appeal to youth and young adult listeners Praise and worship style in white Christian genre (CCM) appealing to those without prior traditional church exposure in word churches, mega ministries, and multicultural churches. Gospel music gains acceptance for scholarly research Hymnals released by black denominations

African-American Historical Timeline and Topics in the Socio-Economic Climate	Black Sacred Music Era	Spiritual Art Form Produced by the Climate	Worship Space	Key Notes and Contributions
Gulf War (Operation Desert Shield) (1990–1991) Magic Johnson announces he is HIV positive (1991) Three-day LA Riots in protest of Rodney King brutality, 50 killed; police acquitted (1992) L. Farrakhan leads Million Man March (1995) More "black first" continue making professional strides in high visibility and influence Ron Brown of the Clinton administration, the first African-American Secretary of Commerce, killed in plane crash in Croatia (1996) OJ Simpson murder trial starts (1995) The Digital Divide affects blacks and socially and economically disadvantaged groups because of less access to practical and life- changing information (mid- 1990s) Cell phones are mainstream for most Americans (mid-1990s) The birth of social media (mid-1990s)	Contemporary period, emerging trends in gospel music business and sound (1990–2000)	Choir and mixed voice ensembles music Cultural and style fusion influences mainstream gospel Inspirational songs emerge *The Free Will Baptist Hymn Book, Rejoice* (1995)	Mainline churches Non-denominational churches Megachurches Multicultural churches Word-based ministries Gospel music industry concerts and festivals Conventions and conferences International, national, regional, and local venues Academia Movie theaters (films/movies)	Gospel music more commercialized Gospel artists with cross-over appeal emerge, some with controversy. These new artists include The Sounds of Blackness, Kirk Franklin, William Becton, Yolanda Adams, Angela and Rene, Take 6, Mary Mary, Kim Burrell, Ben Tankard, and Allen and Allen Other prominent artists of this era: John P. Kee, Hezekiah Walker, Fred Hammond, Marvin Sapp, the Mighty Clouds of Joy, Williams Bros, and Canton Spirituals Collaborative recordings in gospel occur involving artists/producers working together from gospel and secular genres *The Messiah: A Soulful Celebration* produced by Mervyn Warren includes *The Hallelujah Chorus* conducted by Quincy Jones and music produced by George Duke and Patti Austin Jimmy Jam and Terry Lewis produce Yolanda Adams, gospel artist who produced Fred Hammond, Take 6, Richard Smallwood, and others.

African-American Historical Timeline and Topics in the Socio-Economic Climate	Black Sacred Music Era	Spiritual Art Form Produced by the Climate	Worship Space	Key Notes and Contributions
The Internet is mainstream in schools and work and most homes (1999) Smartphones are introduced (1999–2002) Gentrification wave removes black real estate ownership in urban centers				Numerous new artists arrive and gain prominence in the 1990s Yolanda Adams, The Winans, Dynasty, the Clark Family dynasty, Donnie McClurkin, and Mary, Mary are top forerunners alongside Franklin Choirs and ensembles like Kirk Franklin and the Family, Tri-City Singers, Ricky Dillard and New G, and Wilmington Chester Mass Choir and Joe Pace introduce new complexities that require more skilled singers in church More secular artists demonstrate their gospel roots in mainstream music and entertainment venues. *Sister Act II* includes Lauryn Hill's gospel renditions and the *Preacher's Wife* includes Whitney Houston and the Georgia Mass Choir. The soundtrack becomes the best-selling gospel album of all times

African-American Historical Timeline and Topics in the Socio-Economic Climate	Black Sacred Music Era	Spiritual Art Form Produced by the Climate	Worship Space	Key Notes and Contributions
Bush vs. Gore controversial presidential election disenfranchised many blacks and people of color (2000) Al Gore continues global warming and climate change awareness Attack on US led by Osama Bin Laden (Sept 11, 2001) War in Afghanistan starts as a war against terror (2001) Iraq War starts (2003) Same-sex marriage condemned by high profile black ministers (2004) Hurricane Katrina causes death, destruction, and displacement. Major hit to the black community of New Orleans, LA (2005) Housing collapse affects minorities hardest Death of Rosa Parks (2005) Death of Coretta Scott King (2006) Homosexuality addressed in the Black Church after being a forbidden discussion (2007)	Gospel music in the millennium (2000–2017)	Urban contemporary influence Contemporary arrangements for ensemble singing Gospel rap accompanies urban contemporary *African-American Heritage Hymnal* (2001) *The New National Baptist Hymnal—21st Century* captures praise and worship, urban gospel along with traditional, heritage, and spirituals (2001) Praise and worship music genre with gospel influence New Contemporary-influenced congregational anthems composed *Total Praise* hymnal has cross-generational focus (2012)	Mainline churches Non-denominational churches Megachurches Multicultural churches Word-based ministries Gospel music Industry concerts and festivals Conventions and conferences International, national, regional, and local venues Academia Movie theaters (films/movies) Syndicated TV Virtual spaces on the Internet	Israel Houghton and New Breed gains prominence in praise and worship with multicultural appeal. It takes root in the Black Church Kirk Franklin tested the boundaries of gospel music. Accredited with revolutionizing the gospel music industry and innovating music styles and productions Breed introduces a variety of new artists with multicultural appeal amidst business law suits and challenges Gospel rap faced with controversy Gospel music sub-genres within contemporary and traditional emerge Traditional artists seek to maintain relevance by collaborating or by evolving their sound. (Melvin Williams, Shirley Caesar and John P Kee) *Sunday Best* reality TV Show produced by Kirk Franklin launches new solo artists (2007–2015)

African-American Historical Timeline and Topics in the Socio-Economic Climate	Black Sacred Music Era	Spiritual Art Form Produced by the Climate	Worship Space	Key Notes and Contributions
Emergency economic bailout of auto industry (2008) President Obama's historic election as the first black president inspires people of all colors (2008) Death of Michael Jackson (2009) Black in America series on CNN Social media is mainstream Black megachurches in most major cities with a sizeable black community Blacks involved in another gentrification wave; some gain wealth Obamacare enacted (2010) President Obama orders Navy Seal mission to kill Osama Bin Laden (2011) Mid-2000s smartphones are mainstream Death of Whitney Houston (2012)				New generation and millennium of artists include Kiara Sheard, J Moss, Deitrick Haddon, Lacrae, Ty Tribbett, VaShawn Mitchell, James Fortune, William McDowell, Ernest Pugh, L'Andria Johnson, Da Truth, Canton Jones, The Walls, Bryan Andrew Wilson, Jakeylin Carr, Jonathan McReynolds, Casey J, Anita Wilson, Crystal Rucker, Dominique Jones, Tasha Cobbs, Cross Movement, Isaac Caree, JJ Hairston and Youthful Praise, Charles Jenkins, Tasha Page-Lockhart, Travis Green, Anthony Brown and Group TherAPy, Bryan Popin, and Tamela Mann Several new white artists gain contemporary gospel appeal: Martha Munizzi, Vicki Yohe, and Wes Morgan and currently Bryan Popin, who is at the top of the charts (October 2017) Solo artists gain prominence in the industry and dominate the airwaves
Mass shootings and home-grown terrorism become a new public safety threat in America				Numerous gospel artists release praise and worship music that appeals to the Black Church

African-American Historical Timeline and Topics in the Socio-Economic Climate	Black Sacred Music Era	Spiritual Art Form Produced by the Climate	Worship Space	Key Notes and Contributions
Black Lives Matter Movement against racial profiling and police brutality (2013) Military Intervention against ISIL (2014–present) Black Millennials help close the Digital Divide STEM emphasized in underserved and under-represented communities Inclusive theology for LGBTs emerges in the Black Church (2014) White Supremacist murders the Charleston 9 at Emmanuel AME (2015) Confederate flag removed from SC Capitol following the Charleston 9 church massacre Death of Prince (2016) National distress and division caused by Trump presidential win despite verbal attacks against women, people of color, and the disabled White supremacist public protests and racially charged speech increase during Trump presidency				Gospel Artists contenders in awards and recognition across genres Lacrae's music transcends gospel and reigns among the top rap music in the music industry (2012–2013) Gospel music and the Black Church used in the plot of prime-time TV shows (*Greenleaf* and reality TV shows like *Preachers of LA*, *Preachers of ATL*, *Preachers of Detroit*, *Fix My Choir*, *The Manns*, and *Mary Mary*) Gospel artists on prime time and mainstream talk shows

African-American Historical Timeline and Topics in the Socio-Economic Climate	**Black Sacred Music Era**	**Spiritual Art Form Produced by the Climate**	**Worship Space**	**Key Notes and Contributions**
National Museum of African-American History and Culture opens in DC (2016) Biblical prophecy of the solar eclipse fulfilled (August 2017) Series of natural disasters cause death, destruction, and displacement in US, Mexico, Puerto Rico, and other Caribbean islands; California Fires (Fall 2017) US and North Korean tensions NFL players blasted by Trump for kneeling during anthem in protest to police violence against blacks and people of color, pro Black Lives Matter (Fall 2017) Las Vegas massacre re-kindles gun control conversations (Fall 2017)				

How Did We Get to the Current State of Worship in the Collective Black Church?

From a spiritual perspective, African-American worship was birthed from Western influence and oppression in the religious practices of enslaved Africans. Native elements were discouraged, yet a few remained, creating a new unique worship style for Africans in America. Socio-economic injustices have been confronted with the spiritual empowerment afforded by Christianity. As the collective Black Church evolved (inclusive of those outside mainline churches), there has been a greater thirst for relevance for transformed lives. This thirst has been driven by the day-to-day marginalization faced by the African-American minority in the US. This has required collective spiritual growth and maturity in faith. Churches in the black community are faced with the challenge of addressing the growing gap between relevance and what is needed for abundant living and transformation.

The data from Pew Research mentioned earlier in this chapter reveal that faith continues to be important to African-Americans. History has demonstrated that a strong faith has freed us by an emancipation, broken the chains of segregation, sustained us through the great migration and lives lost by assassination, kept us despite mass and often profiled incarceration, and celebrated Obama's inauguration, which was followed by a current state of desolation; yet there is still hope for transformation.

Walking by faith and not by sight has been the compass that has brought us to where we are. More circumstances are occurring that require more commitment and spiritual grounding from those who execute ministry. Faith needs a stronger foundation and girding to counteract what we see. Excellence in gifting and equipping for ministry and spiritual readiness to share an inspiring word are needed to sustain hope in the perilous times we face today.

Music ministry has gone outside the four walls of the church. For gospel music, it was birthed out of a mingling of spiritual testimony across secular music. Gospel music alongside other forms of Christian music has afforded a celebrity lifestyle for many. Record label businesses operate based on ambitious goals and performance metrics. Some artists can leverage their celebrity and popularity platform for the good of Christianity and betterment of humankind. Unfortunately for many Christian artists on major labels, the number of souls saved and the number of lives transformed are not at the top of the vital metrics discussed in the boardroom. Yet in the institution of church, these are the metrics that measure our effectiveness of discipleship. It's not the number of people in the choir, the amount of offering given, nor the number of people in the pews. It is purely the number of conversions we make and sustain to carry out the Great Commission.

The worship we demonstrate in our daily living and in our corporate worship settings positions the opportunity to transact salvation. Therefore, equipping to serve in the music and arts ministry must reach beyond knowing the hottest new releases and most popular music on the airwaves. The repertoire must meet the needs of the worshipers and not the favorite of a select few. Africans brought participatory music to America and it has continued in some form until today but took a back seat in our worship service after groups and ensembles took the forefront. This occurred when the gospel music industry and local gospel circuit evolved during the Golden Age of Gospel (1945–1960s). The congregation became spectators and did not do most of the singing in the service. The praise and worship genre revived the concept of congregational singing, call, and response style.

From a cultural perspective, the commercialization of Christian music and other aspects of Christian culture such as reality TV and film puts the message at risk of theological compromise and can provide a diluted or inaccurate interpretation of the Word. The artistic skill needed to replicate some selections can be beyond the capabilities of the music and arts ministry participants. These aspects create cultural desires in the church to be like what is seen and heard in these commercial products. Motifs must remain to worship Him in spirit and in truth and not based on what is popular. The intent is to deliver the gospel in the message of the music. Some gospel music is inspiring and soothing but not the best at conveying the scriptures of the gospel. As a result, those who lead ministry at the local church must be equipped to discern what is most appropriate from all perspectives. Church sizes range from small scale congregations with limited budgets to mega ministry with multiple campuses. In all arenas of ministry, not just music and arts, those who participate require more commitment to stretch their abilities. The demands have caused some churches to replace choirs with smaller ensembles or praise and worship bands. Smaller churches with limited resources will have to decide how to retain members against the mega ministry and larger churches that render production level services. They will have to be more strategic in promoting their strengths of having church in an intimate setting.

Do You Know the Past of Your Local Church and How It Has Shaped Your Present?

After reading this section and hearing it facilitated in discussion, hopefully you see how we (the Black Church as a whole) got to where we are. The next task is to see how your local church got to where it is today, historically and spiritually. This task can also be applied to each of us individually. As you reflect on the historical journey, the traditions, practices, mentalities, and spirituality should reveal the varied musical pallets most engaging in your setting. You may find that some aspects of your current state are stuck in a prior era or that gaps exist that need closure to enable growth. The journey forward starts with realizing how we got to where we are. The next chapter is a deeper dive into the present state of the Black Church.

Interactive Learning Activity:

Talk to the elder members of the church who have been there the longest. Find out what they recall from the music ministry as far back as they can remember. Understand how the ministry was organized, what activities occurred, and what songs were favored along the way. Learn how music ministry was significant to the church and the changing times of the eras noted in the historical outline of the Black Church.

References

America's changing religious landscape. (2014). *PewForum.org*. Retrieved from http://www.pewforum.org/2015/05/12/americas-changing-religious-landscape/

Arnold-McFarland, A. M. (2016). *The evolution of African-American worship: from music ministry to music industry, as pursued by the independent gospel artist, from the Thomas Dorsey to the Kirk Franklin era*. Raleigh, NC: Eflat Major Publishing. Retrieved from https://issuu.com/eflatmajorpublishing/docs/research_project_-_dmin_-_creative_

Briggs, D. (2015). Are black Americans the most religious and virtuous of all? *HuffingtonPost.com*. Retrieved from https://www.huffingtonpost.com/david-briggs/are-black-americans-the-m_b_6769296.html

Christianity: The story of Africa. (2014). *BBC World Service*. Retrieved from http://www.bbc.co.uk/worldservice/africa/features/storyofafrica/index_section8.shtml

Coffman, E. (2008). What does history say about the first Christians of Africa? *Christianity Today*. Retrieved from http://www.christianitytoday.com/history/2008/august/what-does-history-say-about-first-christians-of-africa.html

Costen, M. (1993). *African-American Christian worship*. Nashville: Abingdon Press.

Davis, L. S. (2012–2015). Various research discussions on Black sacred music.

Davis, L. S. (2015, November). Chicago, roots in gospel music parts 1 and 2. (A. Arnold-McFarland, Interviewer)

GIA Publications, Inc. (2001). African-American heritage hymnal. Chicago: GIA Publications, Inc.

Mellowes, M. (2010). God in America: the Black Church. *PBS*. Retrieved from http://www.pbs.org/godinamerica/black-church/

A religious portrait of African-Americans (from 2007 US Religious Landscape Survey). (2009). *PewForum.org*. Retrieved from http://www.pewforum.org/2009/01/30/a-religious-portrait-of-african-americans/

Stetzer, E. D., & Dates, C. (2016). The exchange—what we can learn from the Black Church when we are pushed to the margins. *ChristianityToday.com*. Retrieved from http://www.christianitytoday.com/edstetzer/2016/august/what-we-can-learn-from-black-church-when-we-are-pushed-to-m.html

Wise, R. D. (2002). Defining African-American gospel music by tracing its historical and musical development from 1900–2000. Retrieved from https://etd.ohiolink.edu/pg_10?0::NO:10:P10_ACCESSION_NUM:osu1243519734

"Worship." (2015). *Merriam-Webster*. Retrieved from https://www.merriam-webster.com/dictionary/worship

CHAPTER THREE

Defining our Present: Worship Challenges in the Black Church

What Is Worship?

Before we can understand worship challenges in the present state of our local church, we must be reminded of what worship is, where it happens, and how we prepare for it. In the general sense, worship is bowing down and submitting to a chosen god. As believers in Christ, we are all called to worship God in our lifestyle and in our daily walk. Worship is not limited to worship services at church. It can occur anywhere and is demonstrated outwardly and inwardly. This was discussed in detail in Chapter One.

A worship service is a public corporate worship of believers. Your preparation is evidence of your commitment. To prepare, what do you need to do mentally? Physically? Spiritually? What resources, logistics, and planning are required to properly prepare? The answers to these questions vary depending on your role in the service. Worship is not just for the pastor and those in the music and arts ministry. All who have a role in the execution of the service and all who attend, even those who are sitting in the congregation, should have a worship preparation plan. We are all members of the body of Christ. Every member of the body of Christ is important, and worship is a display of our commitment to the body (1 Corinthians 12:12–27; Romans 12:3–8).

The Command to Sing Praises

The Bible speaks of using music to worship God. All worshipers, not just those in the choir or on the praise and worship team, are commanded to sing unto the Lord a new song (Psalm 149:1). We are also to admonish one another in psalms, hymns, and spiritual songs (Colossians 3:16). The command to sing and praise our Lord is in numerous scriptures. See Proverbs 96:1, 98:1, and the all-favorite Psalm 150. Take a moment to read these scriptures and reflect on how you have responded to this command.

Why Is the Music and Worship Arts Ministry Vulnerable to Division?

To understand the music and worship arts ministry's vulnerability to division, we must first understand the fall of Lucifer. Some theologians and biblical scholars discuss how God appointed and anointed Lucifer as lead angel, as an appointed worshiper. The association between Lucifer and music is a contested belief by scholars because it is only mentioned once in Ezekiel and no other references in the Bible validate it. However, it makes logical sense when we look at how music can be misused in the world. If one who is admired has dangerous pride, the appeal of his or her artistry and abilities victimizes the less spiritually mature, making these unfortunate individuals vulnerable and blind to the sinful ways of artists they admire.

You can find more on this topic from Steve Ford (2009) in *Is Your Music Department Ministry or Misery* and his discussion on prima-donnas. Also, Rev. Barry Griffing of Zion Song Ministries (2013) discusses the biblical qualifications of appointed worshipers on his site, *International Worship Symposium.* In his discussion of God's due order, he refers to Ezekiel 28 12–19 and Isaiah 14:12—15, where Lucifer is described prior to his fall from his position in heaven. This has been interpreted to mean that his musical abilities were perfectly skillful and he was birthed with the ability to produce vocal pipes and timbrel instrumentation from within. As a musician, this is amazing and hard to comprehend—it is beyond my natural understanding. He could hold down all vocal harmony and music without other singers and a band. Yet I am glad I know that this appeal is what he used to kill, steal, and destroy the fleet of angels. Admiring him was forbidden fruit, and he tempted other angels to draw near to him. He convinced one third of the angels to follow him. They, along with Lucifer, lost their souls because they stood in awe of him instead of continuing in awe of the God, who had given him these skills. Their awe of Lucifer allowed him to infiltrate their thinking. Lucifer had been in close fellowship with God prior to his fall. This fall resulted from his pride and desire to make himself a god. He displayed traits that will destroy a music ministry, divide a church, and badly influence popular music of the world.

Lucifer will never again have the opportunity we have to worship and dwell with God. He is a disgruntled employee on the outside looking in, still trying to plant mental poison to destroy seeds of growth in those still employed by the body of Christ. His work history in ministry allows him to know how to manipulate the music ministry to create division, distractions, and ineffectiveness. For this reason, it is imperative that those who enter music ministry as a vocalist, musician, or participant in other segments of worship arts (dance, drama, audio, and production support) fervently seek spiritual wisdom and discernment, remain in constant fellowship with God, and keep a humble and teachable spirit. All this is necessary to overcome spiritual attacks.

Churches have a role in making sure they do not create an atmosphere for a divisive or proud spirit to develop in the music ministry, with the pastor, or with other leadership in the church. Reference these scriptures on accountability for further understanding to help safeguard the ministry: Proverbs 27:17; Galatians 6:1–2; Matthew 18:15–17; James 5:16; and Ephesians 4:1–32.

Worship in Spirit and Truth

As mentioned in Chapter One, the Levites in the Old Testament were appointed to sing and play the instruments after being sanctified and examined for a period of time. Reference these scriptures: 1 Chronicles 28: 11–19; 16:27; 25:6–8; 15:22.

In Exodus 32, the Levites remained loyal to Moses and to God's instructions when the Israelites chose to worship a golden calf while Moses was on Mt. Sinai. In Hebrew *Levi* means "joined" as in a pledge of loyalty. The Levites were so loyal that they killed their own relatives who had sinned against God. Those who lead the worship of God publicly must be consistently girded and loyal to the Word to be effective. This loyalty and pledge to God sets the spirit of unity in the musical display of worship. Achieving this loyalty is the key to overcoming all other worship challenges and prevents the rise of a "Lucifer-like" spirit of pride, self-gratification, arrogance, envy, and manipulation.

Volunteer participation in music and worship arts ministry without demonstration of spiritual readiness and maturity opens the possibility for vulnerability. Spiritual maturity is more important than natural skill. As we can see, Lucifer was perfect, attractive, appealing, and talented, yet the sole cause of downfall. The most talented and gifted singers and musicians are not necessarily appropriate for your music ministry if their heart does not have the right motives. A selection process is seen as unfair or discriminating, yet without it the music ministry runs the risk of putting manmade qualifications above what God has prescribed in His Word. Using a volunteer choir with no selection criteria is a manmade concept. We are called to worship God in spirit and in truth. To do this, we have to know what truth is. Tradition does not equal truth. The truth is not always kind. It does not always align with our personal beliefs, values, motives, and feelings. The truth is what God's Word tells us we need to do and not what we want to do because of tradition. Tradition is what has always existed and what our cultural norms are. God's requirements of those who lead His people and of those who are appointed to a position are strict and require them to show themselves approved (2

Timothy 2:15). Is the worship at your church in spirit and in truth? Read Isaiah 29:13 and John 4:23–24.

The Root of Challenges in Music and Worship Arts Ministry Today

All churches, regardless of dominant ethnicity, can expect to experience challenges in their worship and music ministry if spiritual and technical abilities are lacking. Worship challenges occur when there is a lack of unity and a loss of focus on glorifying God. If the structure does not align with the biblical model to appoint lead worshipers (singers, musicians, etc.), the ministry will remain vulnerable to a variety of difficulties. Volunteer and hired participants alike should have spiritual and music guidelines, protocol, expectations, and grounds for dismissal. A lack of scripturally-aligned entry processes does not lay a good foundation for effectively operating and growing a music and worship arts ministry.

At a minimum, our commitment to achieving excellence in the music and worship ministry should be no less than what we provide to sport teams, school bands and orchestras, scout groups, fraternities, sororities, workplaces, and other organizations to which we willingly submit. We accept the requirement of selection and try out for these manmade organizations but reject it when we need to apply it to our worship. This is the root of our challenge in the music and worship arts ministry today.

A Survey of Worship in the Local Church

During Gospel Music One Sound Project in November 2015, I conducted a survey called "Music Ministry Development" to gauge the present state and effectiveness of worship in the Raleigh-Durham area. It was targeted at identifying current issues faced in local black churches and community music ministries of gospel music (Arnold-McFarland A. M., 2015–2017).

The collected data aided in understanding the present state of the African-American worship experience (Arnold-McFarland A. M., 2016). A random sample was used of 29 anonymous participants who completed 17 questions. The survey was posted on Gospel Music One Sound Project Facebook page and circulated by email to my musician and pastoral contacts, primarily in the Raleigh-Durham, North Carolina, area. They had various roles in the church music ministry including ministry of music, choir director, worship leader, praise and worship band member, gospel artist, staff musician, staff minister, and senior pastor. The church sizes were primarily 300 members or less with one to two services per Sunday. Various ones had oversight of a youth/young adult choir, male choir, some form of an adult mix voice, or a praise team.

One of the questions specifically focused on the challenges that hinder the growth of the music ministry and worship arts, vehicles for public worship. The participants were allowed to choose multiple responses. Approximately 60% of the top responses are highlighted in red below.

What challenges hinder the growth of your music ministry/worship arts? Check all that apply.

Answer Options	Response Percent	Response Count
Finding musical staff that will stay long term (5 years or more)	3.3%	7
Being able to get rid of musical staff members not willing to grow with the ministry	1.9%	4
Finding the right skill set to help the music ministry to grow	5.1%	11
The Min of Music/Music Director/Staff Musicians do not have a good relationship with the Pastor	0.5%	1
Setting a budget that will retain the right skill sets for the music	6.0%	13
Need to improve on equipment, sound system, microphones, instruments and tools for execution	3.7%	8
To much reliance on volunteer support without a developing others	3.3%	7
Competition among the choirs, choir members, musicians, church leaders	1.9%	4
No succession planning in leadership of the music ministry to continue when people leave	3.7%	8
Choir members participate in various other ministries with overlapping commitments	6.5%	14
Budget does not include additional seminars for choir members	5.6%	12
Exposing choir members to vocal development, seminars, etc. outside of rehearsal time	8.8%	19
No vision or plan for growth in the music ministry	5.1%	11
Lack of capabilities within the music ministry to meet the expectations of the choir	1.4%	3
Consistency in choir member participation	5.6%	12
Getting choir members to practice outside of rehearsal	8.4%	18
Finding repertoire that is within the capability of the choir	4.2%	9
Participation and attendance of rehearsal	4.7%	10
Lack of spiritual growth and immaturity deters participation	3.3%	7
Lack of spiritual growth affects interest and motivation to grow	4.2%	9
Lack of strategic planning to grow the music ministry support with the church	2.8%	6
Lack of unity in the choir	3.3%	7
Music ministry/worship arts needs motivation	3.7%	8
Need better coordination between music, dance, media to have more effective delivery	2.8%	6
Other (please explain)	0.5%	1
	100.0%	215
answered question		29
skipped question		0

Source: **Arnold-McFarland, A.M. (2015–2017). Gospel Music One Sound Project**

In October 2016, a follow-up inquiry occurred among a small focus group of gospel music ministry colleagues of 20 years or more in churches of the Raleigh-Durham, North Carolina, area. In an interview format or electronic conversational format, they individually provided their assessment of the top issues they anticipate facing in the next 5–10 years. These are listed in order of concern based on the current situation (Arnold-McFarland A. M., 2015–2017).

Talent

- Gap exist in talent/capability of choir to sing current music from the gospel music industry
- Staff needs ongoing development and audio and media support
- No space left for other art forms in worship

Spiritual Growth

- Choir, praise team, and staff deficient in spiritual understanding of role and purpose in music ministry (choir, praise team, staff)
- Choir members not open to change and resist growth

Repertoire

- More diverse appeal and balance in style of music needed
- Rich heritage of hymns, spirituals, note singing becoming obsolete
- Message in the music not always scripturally sound

Youth/Young Adults

- Youth choir losing interest and lacking motivation
- Youth desires their own style in praising God (more youthful)
- Young adults lack interest in traditional worship; need relevance

Budget

- No budget provided for growing demands to support the church growth
- No investment made in seminars/training

Vision/Strategy

- Minister of music not empowered to pace change and growth
- Structured planning for music ministry lacking
- Succession planning missing

In 2017, I did not conduct another survey, yet a major observation I made was the slow awareness and even resistance to versatility, diversity and flexibility (Arnold-McFarland A. M., 2015 - 2017).

Versatility/Diversity/Flexibility

- A plan is needed to address changing demographics of the church and how the music and worship arts ministry should respond.
- Churches are challenged to have service flow and music that appeals to different generations. Seniors want to hear more hymns and traditional music. Young adults and some mid-life adults like contemporary music and a contemporary style of service. How can churches best minister multi-generationally?
- Smaller ministries are still not equipped for remote worship or even different service times. Guidance on how to grow in technology and toward music and worship arts is needed.

For the Black Church, the demographics of their location may be changing, and those who enter their doors may not be familiar faces or relatives of people in the church. They may have an urban style. They could be dressed down and wearing tattoos or body piercings. They may be homeless or a part of the LGBTQ community. They might even be a different ethnicity or speak English as a second language. Amidst these differences, the music and worship arts ministry will have to meet the needs of the people. Song selection will have to be strategic, and it may not be the hottest new hit on the radio.

There is a growing challenge for multi-generational appeal. Seniors and baby boomers are spiritually fulfilled by hymns and old favorite traditional music. Generation Xers were children of hymns yet grew up on choir music of the modern contemporary era. Millennials may be children of parents who did not grow up in church, so their awareness of traditional music and hymns may be limited. They may connect more with urban contemporary and praise and worship genres.

Pew Research (The Pew Forum on Religion and Public Life, 2014) shows a growing trend toward non-denominational worship. Traditional and denominational churches are losing members to contemporary style services or worship space. Having worship and ministry versatility will help retain millennials and even some Generation Xers whose busy lives find this flow of service more fitting and relevant.

Black churches who are victim to the digital divide need to become "digitally divine." They need to include technology in their vision, beyond the music and worship arts ministry. In the millennium, it will be difficult to grow without being comfortable with a reasonable level of digital presence: a functional website, online giving, email use, live stream, and social media.

Some churches believe this is not important because many of their members are seniors who do not use nor have access to the Internet. The church should offer training in this area and perhaps have a technology initiative. People who do not have some level of computer or mobile device literacy will be affected in other areas of their well-being.

A new set of skills and talent is needed to produce a quality display of music, dance, and other artistic performances both in person and live stream. Qualified staff in worship technology should have skills in sound/audio, media projection, lighting, and video. To execute effectively, their skills should be coordinated by a stage or production manager. This is the reason I have added *worship arts* alongside music ministry in this book. To survive and evolve in relevance, the mind-set must be beyond music.

If churches do not become equipped for flexible methods of worship, operation, and communication, they will never make space for the next generation. Future generations will continue to worship elsewhere or not at all. Using flexible methods does not mean presenting a flexible message. We must continue to worship in spirit and in truth, despite the changing dynamics among worshipers. The message must maintain integrity, and the service must set the atmosphere for deliverance from the struggles and issues affecting lives today.

Interactive Learning Activity:

This is a representation of churches that have similar criteria as those who participated in the survey. As you ponder this chapter, take notice of the areas that resonate with you and your ministry. Conduct your own research to assess the present state of worship at your church. See the questionnaire below.

How Do I Define the Present State of the Music and Worship Arts Ministry in My Church?

Before improvements can be made in the effectiveness of your music and worship arts ministry, you must understand what is happening currently to foster the worship experience at your church. In this step, gain a high level of understanding of the comprehensive music and worship arts ministry. Do not get into the details; just understand how "the railroad runs" as it exists today. Imagine you are explaining this to someone who is not familiar with the church and align with those involved on a high-level summary. As a consultant, this is the type of conversation I have with the pastor and music ministry leaders to gain a general understanding of where they are.

Here are questions to help you:

1) Describe the choirs, ensembles, and support teams in your music and worship arts ministry.
2) How many participants do you have?
3) What expectations and guidelines exist for participation?
4) What is the process for preparation for worship service, both collectively and individually?
5) What are the roles and responsibilities of key leaders?
6) How is music selected?
7) What is the typical repertoire and style of each choir/ensemble?
8) Describe the flow of service.
9) What selections are the church's top favorites?
10) What are the mission and vision statement of the music and worship arts ministry?
11) How does communication occur?
12) Where are your music files, key documents, and library stored?
13) What are the top few challenges faced by the music and worship arts ministry and by the church as a whole?
14) Describe any situations that have occurred that created unique challenges or roadblocks?
15) What are the key components of the budget? (Musical staff salaries, robes, education, equipment maintenance, new purchase, hymnals/music, etc.)

References

America's changing religious landscape (2014). *PewForum.org*. Retrieved from http://www.pewforum.org/2015/05/12/americas-changing-religious-landscape/

Arnold-McFarland, A. M. (2016). *The evolution of African-American worship: from music ministry to music industry, as pursued by the independent gospel artist, from the Thomas Dorsey to the Kirk Franklin era*. Raleigh, NC: Eflat Major Publishing. Retrieved from https://issuu.com/eflatmajorpublishing/docs/research_project_-_dmin_-_creative_

Arnold-McFarland, A.M. (2015–2017). Gospel Music One Sound Project.

Ford, S. (2009). *Is your music department ministry or misery?* Middletown: S. Ford Music Publishing.

Griffing, B. R. (2013). Biblical qualifications of appointed worshipers. *International Worship Symposium*. Retrieved from http://www.internationalworshipsymposium.org/Article003.html

CHAPTER FOUR

Your Music and Worship Arts Ministry: Measuring and Assessing Your Present Challenges

What Present Challenges Exist in Your Music and Worship Arts Ministry?

Once you have defined your present state, your next step is to gain insight on the problems that exist today. In this step you are taking a deeper look to understand details that contribute to challenges. It is best to approach this from the perspective of all those who have a stake, a need, a role, or a desire to improve the worship experience. A comprehensive approach includes the congregation, the pastor, the musicians, the praise and worship team, the choir members, the sound and audio ministry, lighting and projection team members, and those who are served (Arnold-McFarland A. M., 2017).

You can create a survey, conduct interviews as one-on-one conversations, or have focus group discussions to gain deeper insight to the current state of the worship experience in your church. Some people may choose to do a combination of some or all of these methods of observation. Collect profile information on the participants so you can compare that with their responses. Names are not necessary, but you do need general information on their traits (gender, ethnicity, denomination, age group, marital status, Christian experience, church activities/positions, etc.). Your goal is to understand opinions, what is working well, what is not working well, and what ideas exist to make improvements. Keep in mind that opinions are based on various perspectives, and they are not necessarily facts. Even if you disagree with an opinion, it is important to understand the differences of opinion (Arnold-McFarland A. M., 2017).

Conducting a Survey

If you choose to do a survey, here are some guidelines to help you conduct it. If you do not have a lot of experience in facilitating a survey, it is best to get coaching from someone who understands survey creation and facilitation techniques. You can also research survey tools and best practices and guidelines online. A tool I use called Survey Monkey offers free use for a limited number of questions. My services are also available to help with your survey.

1) Compile questions to get feedback on the worship experience of your sample. It's easiest to use an online data collection tool for ease of analytics. If you have to use paper copies, the results can be entered later into an electronic tool.
2) Obtain a randomly selected mixed representation that is proportionate to the full population of the roles. The larger the sample size, the less margin of error you will have in conclusions you draw from the sample. The sample represents the target population (congregation, choir, musicians, pastor, etc., mentioned above). A general rule is to get at least 30 participants. If you have a small church, a convenient sample may be the best you can do.
3) Ensure people answer the survey completely and go back to them for missing information if the source can be traced. Keep the individual responses confidential.
4) Analyze the results for common trends, compare for differences, and look for problems identified.

Using a SWOT Analysis With a Focus Group

Assessing your present state starts with collecting data via surveys, observations, and targeted interviews or by using a strategic tool such as a SWOT Analysis. This is a business tool that uses qualitative/attribute data to help put measures on the current state of an assessed situation. It is used in strategic planning for a project or business venture or by individuals to assess the current position toward achieving an objective or goal. It categorizes current stated data into strengths (advantages), weaknesses (disadvantages), opportunities (unused benefits), and threats (trouble and disruptions) that exist toward reaching a goal or a considered venture. This is an easy tool I often use to collect and organize current state data on music ministries at local churches. This tool can be used to measure quantitatively and evaluate each entity in the music ministry. Each choir/entity can do a SWOT on their specific group. For a more in-depth perspective, it can be used at the vocal section level (i.e., sopranos, altos, tenors, baritone/bass separately in the same choir) (Arnold-McFarland A. M., 2015—2017).

Subgroups are established to complete a SWOT Analysis template as shown below for their specific choir. One person is identified to scribe the results for their subgroup. The amount of time allotted depends on the size of the small groups. For example, if each group has three to five people, it typically takes 30 minutes. See the example below.

Objective—to increase choir member retention across all choirs

First Christian Church

What will help us achieve this?	What will prevent us from achieving this?
Strengths • Our choir has good fellowship and comradery. • Most choir members have been faithful for a number of years. • Choir members are open minded and teachable. • We have strong harmony.	**Weaknesses** • The new repertoire does not fit everyone's abilities. • No written guidelines. • Choir members do not retain what has been taught in prior rehearsals. • Many people travel during the summer months.
Opportunities • We could combine choirs in the summer months to increase representation and unity. • We could take one month off and have congregational singing or just the praise team. • We could plan a schedule of committed Sundays per month, so we can plan music accordingly. • On special services, we can invite the congregation to participate and possibly join as new members.	**Threats** • Choir members could burn out from over-commitment in multiple ministries. • The new musician could take another position at another church. • We are instrument dependent and have no acapella songs or soundtracks. • Young adults do not return to sing after they graduate from high school, and we have not made plans to stay connected with them. • No spiritual growth is evident.

Compile All Data Collected

All data collected from any surveys, interviews, or SWOTs are compiled and evaluated qualitatively to gauge thought and current opinions. The discussion generated allows gaps in understanding, misalignments, and expectations to be revealed. Organizing the data into a spreadsheet is suggested so it can easily be sorted, viewed, and analyzed from different perspectives. List all findings and combine any repeat responses. At this point, we have only completed the list of gaps and action items we want to sustain or leverage, and we've identified which ministry entity is affected (Arnold-McFarland A. M., 2017).

Sample Gap Analysis and Improvement Template

Gaps & Action Items	SWOT	Gospel Choir	Youth Choir	Male Choir	Action for Closure	Focus Area	Milestone Improvement	Phase	Assignees	Date
No new repertoire	W	X	X	X						
Tardiness	W	X	X							
Vocal Ability	W		X							
No written guidelines	W	X	X	X						
Musician quits	T	X	X	X						
No Rehearsals	T	X	X	X						
No spiritual growth is evident	T	X	X	X						
Good fellowship	S	X		X						
We have strong harmony	S	X								
Teachable Choir	S		X							

References

Arnold-McFarland A. M. (2015—2017). Gospel Music One Sound Project.

Arnold-McFarland, A. M. (2017). Moving forward and facing the future (music and worship seminar, Christian Home Christian Church). Apex, NC: Eflat Major Productions.

CHAPTER FIVE

Self-Analysis: How Do We Face Our Future?

How Do You Face the Future?

Facing your future starts with facing where you are today. Once your local church has completed data collection and observations of your present state, the next step is to analyze the data and interpret what it is telling you. Accepting the results of the analysis is the first step in facing where you stand today. The analysis compares the current with the projected future and reveals what needs to happen to reach your goals for the future. You will need to look at the results of the analysis for trends, themes, possibilities, and gaps to close (Arnold-McFarland A. M., 2017).

What Is the Outlook for the Future?

Facing the future requires knowledge of what the future needs to look like. Usually the leadership already has some vision of what the future should hold. The vision of the music and worship arts ministry must line up with the vision of the church, yet it will speak directly to those involved in music and worship arts. The vision provides a mental picture of what the future looks like. Fulfillment of the vision should begin to evolve during the analyzing phase. The data analytics dictates the next best steps toward that vision, based on the insight and diagnosis gained from data (Arnold-McFarland A. M., 2017).

Establish Grounds Rules

As a consultant, my role is to facilitate the analysis step with the ministry, as it can often be difficult to discuss what the data reveals. This is when critical issues become evident. It is imperative to have ground rules on how this discussion will go.

1) No one person is at fault, and being judgmental will not help us propel the ministry forward.
2) We are agreeing to move forward together.
3) We will discuss our shortcomings to understand root causes and to work toward a solution.
4) The facilitator will manage the discussion and determine if a separate conversation is warranted.
5) Let us review the fruit of the Spirit together and abide by them in our discussion. "But the fruit of the Spirit is love, joy, peace, longsuffering, kindness, goodness, faithfulness, gentleness, self-control. Against such there is no law" (Galatians 5:22–23).

The Analysis Process

In the analysis process, I reference the compiled data from the prior chapter that came from various sources (i.e., surveys, interviews, focus groups, SWOT Analysis, and other strategy or analysis tools). This information allows us to gain insight, current thoughts, and data-based opinions. In this phase, if we realize quick solutions or ideas on items, we can go ahead and write these down and include them in the analysis and improvement spreadsheet. If the list is long, the participants can agree on criteria to help filter the list down to the vital few actions, based on criticality and urgency.

One method for filtering is to evaluate impact versus effort. The group may choose to focus on items that have high impact with low effort. This does not mean that those requiring high effort and high impact would not be tackled. Further analysis and offline discussion may be needed to address these. Critical items need more in-depth analysis before conclusions for next steps can be determined (Arnold-McFarland A. M., 2017).

Interactive Learning Activity:

The completion of this analysis of the choir or other entity presents an opportune time for each individual to do a self-analysis to identify areas for personal growth and development. Once we have faced ourselves as a choir, we must also be willing to have accountability and face our own shortcomings. This can be done by first doing a self-check and then getting feedback from our ministry leaders.

First, ask yourself the questions below. Then ask these same questions of your ministry leader or others who rely on your best effort. This could be your fellow musicians, your fellow vocal section members, your choir director, music director, or ministry of music. Music and worship arts ministry leaders can obtain feedback from their leadership, usually the senior pastor. The pastor can obtain feedback from his or her subordinates. The answers here will help us compile the personal improvement plan in the next chapter. Tactful and honest feedback helps us brings awareness for growth and reveals where there are misalignments and misinterpretations. It provides a basis for direction.

Accountability Questions:

What do I already do well that I need to keep doing?
What do I need to stop doing?

What do I need to do better individually to contribute more effectively to the worship and arts ministry?

We should all be teachable and willing to grow for the good of the ministry. Here are key scriptures to study if you need help in being able to accept feedback and in having a teachable spirit. See what other scriptures address this and memorize them so the Word of truth will be in your heart when you need it.

> Whoever disregards discipline comes to poverty and shame, but whoever heeds correction is honored.
>
> Proverbs 13:18 NIV

> Whoever loves instruction loves knowledge, But he who hates correction *is* stupid.
>
> Proverbs 12:1

> Be diligent to present yourself approved to God, a worker who does not need to be ashamed, rightly dividing the word of truth.
>
> 2 Timothy 2:15

References

Arnold-McFarland, A. M. (2017). Moving forward and facing the future (music and worship seminar, Christian Home Christian Church). Apex, NC: Eflat Major Productions.

CHAPTER SIX

Improving Forward: What Is Our Vision for the Future?

Confirming the Vision of the Future

The next phase is for the collective group and leadership to confirm the vision that demonstrates where they need to be in the next several years. This helps bring clarity to what that vision needs to be. This may not be the long-term vision, yet it is one that is realistic to fulfill within the next one to three years with the help of an improvement team to run with the vision. Establishing a vision statement is a good way to align the ministry and communicate the goal toward which everyone is working. The vision statement is one sentence or phrase that inspires and motivates the vision carriers to reach for it. This is done by completing the detailed tasks that bring about improvements. A series of improvements brings about milestones toward reaching the vision. This happens over time—usually several years (Arnold-McFarland A. M., 2016).

The vision should speak of the future as if the critical gaps are closed, strengths are sustained, threats are minimized, and opportunities have already been leveraged. The impact is known and spoken by the vision. The vision becomes the new truth. The carriers must walk by faith and not by sight, believing that this vision will come to pass. They must not faint before the vision becomes the now.

The Improvement Team

I suggest that an improvement team or small core group be appointed to take over from this point to move the ministry forward with a facilitated and managed project. They will complete the process of identifying remaining needed improvements. They should be a representative cross-section of the music and worship arts ministry.

The improvement team must be carefully selected and has to include members who are spiritual mature enough to carry the vision. These should be individuals with faith strong enough to transform the ministry. They will have to encourage one another not to let progress stall, fall, or die. They should have the natural abilities to organize, plan, and follow through on tasks until completion. This team needs a leader, a project manager, a champion, and/or executive steering team. Generally, the pastor is the champion. As the consultant, I coach the team, get them kicked off, and help them launch the improvement phase. We will have webinars, follow-up sessions, and one-on-one discussions on their segments of the visions. The improvement team reports progress to the champion or steering team.

Here are a few study scriptures to inspire the heralds and vision carriers.

> "For I know the plans I have for you, declares the Lord, plans for welfare and not for evil, to give you a future and a hope."
>
> Jeremiah 29:11 NIV

> Then the Lord answered me and said: "Write the vision and make *it* plain on tablets,
>
> That he may run who reads it. For the vision *is* yet for an appointed time; But at the end it will speak, and it will not lie. Though it tarries, wait for it; because it will surely come, It will not tarry.
>
> Habakkuk 2:2–3

> Where there is no vision, the people perish: but he that keepeth the law, happy is he.
>
> Proverbs 29:18 KJV

> But Jesus looked at *them* and said to them, "With men this is impossible, but with God all things are possible."
>
> Matthew 19:26

> Surely the Lord GOD does nothing, Unless He reveals His secret to His servants the prophets.
>
> Amos 3:7

> As for these four young men, God gave them knowledge and skill in all literature and wisdom; and Daniel had understanding in all visions and dreams.
>
> Daniel 1:17

Moving Forward Means "Improving" Forward

Improvement is demonstrated evidence that moves the ministry in the right direction. Be aware that improvements can occur up to a point where more is not better. When that happens, diminishing returns can stall progress, plateau it, overwhelm the ministry, or even depart from the vision. Be careful not to expect quantity to be more effective than quality. For example, having more choir members does not necessarily improve the quality of the music or of the effectiveness of the choir. Having more songs to sing does not make the choir more effective if the quality in delivering the songs is not effective. Having more rehearsals does not improve readiness if more preparation isn't done to ensure good use of the time. Work smarter and not harder. Improvements should be efficient and value-added and should produce good quality outcomes.

What Actions Will Move Us Forward to Our Future?

In the improvement phase, our goal is to complete the process already started to identify action items needed to move us toward our future. Let me emphasize that improvement is movement toward the vision, which will sustain strengths, close gaps caused by weaknesses, leverage opportunities, and manage risks to prevent threats. These solutions and improvements are added to what has already been started on the analysis and improvement sheet. Some items may require more research and approval for funding before the real solution can be realized. A short-term action may be the immediate solution (Arnold-McFarland A. M., 2017).

Best practices and possible solutions are listed in the quick reference guide in the appendices of this book. These can be leveraged to provide appropriate solutions for the analysis and improvement sheet. The action items are then categorized into milestones based on the prescribed categories in the quick reference chart. A subteam leader is assigned to complete a common set of action items associated with the milestone. The assignees who managing their own small teams are listed first in the assignee column. Their subteam members are improvement team members or others in the ministry who are a good fit for complete the tasks.

Timeline Management

A timeline is compiled to work on planning the execution over the next 90 Days. The execution is positioned for six to nine months. The improvement team should expect to see the vision begin to unfold within one year. The next 90 days are the most critical for success, and a timeline manager or project manager should be assigned the task of keeping the team accountable to the time frame. These items must run in parallel to what is already on the church calendar. The timeline should be made a priority, even if that means adjusting what is on the calendar to position the team for success. Be careful to not overcommit the team, as this add work to their current responsibilities in the church.

Here is an example Gap Analysis and Improvement Template for our discussion.

Gap or Area to Sustain	SWOT	Gospel Choir	Youth Choir	Male Choir	Action for Closure	Focus Area	Milestone Improvement	Phase	Assignees	Date
Tardiness	W	X	X		Set guide-lines	Personnel issues: job fit and performance	Guidelines, roles, and responsibili-ties in place	30–60 days	Miriam: Noah, David, Mary	12/3/17
No written guidelines	W	X	X	X	Set guide-lines	Personnel issues: job fit and performance	Guidelines, roles, and responsibili-ties in place	30–60 days	Miriam: Noah, David, Mary	12/3/17
No rehearsals	T	X	X	X	Set guide-lines	Personnel issues: job fit and performance	Guidelines, roles, and responsibili-ties in place	30–60 days	Miriam: Noah, David, Mary	12/3/17
No spiritual growth evident	T	X	X	X	Attend Bible study and Sunday school	Spiritual maturity	Guidelines, roles, and responsibili-ties in place	30–60 days	Miriam: Noah, David, Mary	12/3/17
Teachable choir	S		X		Add criteria to guide-lines	Spiritual maturity	Spiritual growth demonstrated	90–120 days	Trey: Louise, Maria, Pat	12/3/17
Strong harmony	S	X			Share tech-niques with other choirs	Preparation, repertoire, training, and awareness	Quarterly training seminars scheduled	60–90 days	Tony: Sonya, Lisa, Sarah	12/10/17
New repertoire	W	X	X	X	Search song books and online sources and attend work-shops	Preparation, repertoire, training, and awareness	Five new songs iden-tified and taught to each choir	60–90 days	Tony: Sonya, Lisa, Sarah	1/21/18

Vocal ability	W		X		In-house training	Preparation, repertoire, training, and awareness	Quarterly training seminars scheduled	60–90 days	Tony: Sonya, Lisa, Sarah	2/18/18
Musician quits	T	X	X	X	Have acapella songs, get tracks	Personnel Issues: job fit and performance	Risk manage-ment plan in place	60–90 days	Mike: Sheldon, Ray, Rod	2/18/18
Good fellowship	S	X		X	Plan outreach activities	Commitment and engagement	Fellowship activities planned with outreach	60–90 days	Trey: Louise, Maria, Pat	2/25/18

This table shows milestone initiatives of First Christian Church. To even the load, some subteam owners have multiple milestones.

Milestone Initiative	**Subteam Owner**	**Team Members**
Guidelines, roles, and responsibilities	Miriam	Noah, David, Mary
Evidence of spir-itual growth	Trey	Louise, Maria, Pat
Quarterly training seminars scheduled	Tony	Sonya, Lisa, Sarah
Five new songs iden-tified and taught	Tony	Sonya, Lisa, Sarah
Risk management	Mike	Sheldon, Ray, Rod
Fellowship activities	Trey	Louise, Maria, Pat

After the template is completed, a visual of the milestones, timeline, and vision helps communicate the plan and execution. An example of what the visual looks like for First Christian Church is shown below. The improvement team should be meeting in the planning phase of the project to complete the detailed tasks that will deliver the milestone initiatives. The execution phase reveals how the ministry operates after improvements are implemented.

References

Arnold-McFarland, A. M. (2016). Moving forward and facing the future (lecture presentation, General Baptist State Convention of NC). Raleigh, NC.

Arnold-McFarland, A. M. (2017). Moving forward and facing the future (music and worship seminar, Christian Home Christian Church). Apex, NC: Eflat Major Productions.

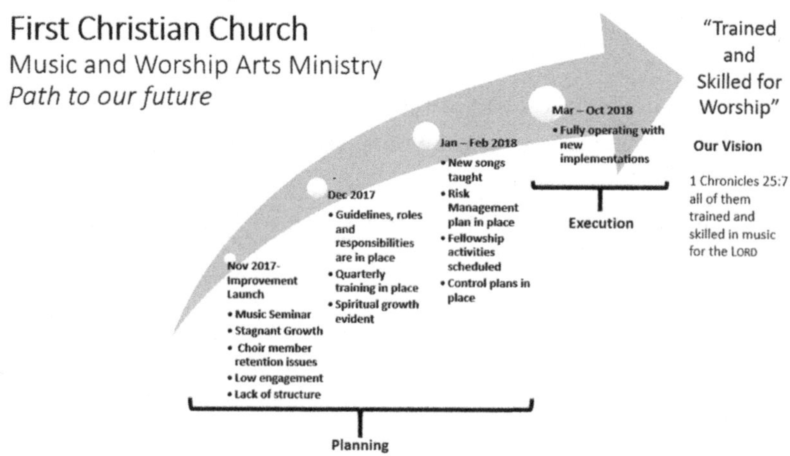

Interactive Learning Activity:

As the ministry grows, the individual participants must be fit spiritually, mentally, and physically for purpose and growth. I highly recommend having each seminar participant write a personal improvement plan; the improvement team should begin this process to set the example. Each team member takes ownership of items in the overall improvement plan, as well as items in his or her self-improvement plan. Reference the self-analysis for personal gaps identified and include them in the personal improvement plans. The music and worship arts leadership can discuss these plans individually with each member to understand developmental needs and to make suggestions for improvement.

- What two or three things can I start doing right away to help the music and worship arts ministry?

  Reference the self- analysis and feedback obtained.

- What two or three things can I start doing right away to help myself grow spiritually and musically?

  How will I better prepare for worship spiritually, mentally, and physically?

  How will I improve my personal practice time?

- What effort and resources are needed to start the personal improvement plan?
- When will I start each item?
- Who will hold me accountable?

CHAPTER SEVEN

Self-Control: Sustaining the Transformation

The improvements implemented to grow the ministry must be sustained with a plan for control. Think of this in the same way God wants us to demonstrate self-control in our spiritual lives for the improvements we make in our spiritual walk. There will be temptations to revert to the old way of thinking and behaving. Spiritual nourishment, encouragement and prayer will be key ingredients of sustaining the transformation (Arnold-McFarland A. M., 2015–2017).

A Control Plan for Sustaining Change

In our practical ministry work, we will need methods to control the new changes. This will require a plan to audit progress and to address movement in the wrong direction. An effective proactive approach to sustain the transformation safeguards the music and worship arts ministry. This is an intentional and documented plan that recognizes when the newly implemented improvements are moving out of control. Determine the indicators of success for those critical components that keep the music and worship arts ministry thriving. Know the limitations (upper and lower levels) that warrant an action so the ministry maintains operational control. The most effective control plan has actions and indicators integrated into the ministry so the plan is self-controlling.

Here is an example of a control plan:

First Christian Church—Music and Worship Arts Control Plan

Milestone Initiative and Owner	**Evidence of Control**	**Integration in Ministry Processes**	**Indicators of Loss of Control**	**Action to Regain Control**
Guidelines, roles, and responsibilities (Miriam)	Guidelines for roles and responsibilities are consistently followed. A regular awareness session happens quarterly to keep participants informed of the state of the ministry. An assessment for updates occurs annually.	Documented performance reviews with feedback for choir members and ministry leaders occurs twice a year. Participants are aware of consequences.	Guidelines, roles, and responsibilities are not consistently followed 30% of the time and the issues go unaddressed by ministry leaders.	Ministry leaders have a mandatory call meeting with participants to review issues affecting adherence to this objective. Actions are put into place to regain control.
Evidence of spiritual growth (Trey)	Ministry participants consistently attend Bible study, Sunday school, and other spiritual growth activities outside of worship service. There is an increase in ministry commitment, discipline, and the fruit of the Spirit.	Ministry participants take turns leading the 15-minute devotional study that precedes each rehearsal. Bible study or Sunday school attendance is required to be in the music and worship arts ministry.	Participants are not consistently attending Bible study or Sunday school 30% of the time and the issue goes unaddressed by the ministry leaders.	Ministry leaders have a mandatory call meeting with participants to review issues affecting adherence to this objective. Actions are put into place to regain control.

Quarterly training seminars scheduled (Tony)	Quarterly training occurs consistently and 90% of the ministry participants attend.	A quarterly training seminar takes place that is mandatory for all participants.	Quarterly training does not occur consistently or participation is less than 75%. Issues go unaddressed by ministry leaders.	Ministry leaders have a mandatory call meeting with participants to review issues affecting adherence to this objective. Actions are put into place to regain control.
Five new songs identified and taught (Tony)	New repertoire is consistently added that is a good fit for the ministry and at a pace appropriate for the capacity.	The new repertoire for the upcoming quarter is pre-planned and communicated three months in advance. Learning aids, practicing tips, recordings, and sectionals occur to maintain good quality in delivery.	The integrated processes are not consistently executed. Participants do not use the mechanisms provided to support learning new songs.	Ministry leaders have a mandatory call meeting with participants to review issues affecting adherence to this objective. Actions are put into place to regain control.
Risk Management (Mike)	A risk management plan for items such as substitute staff, remote rehearsing options, and acapella songs is documented and has been executed.	Ministry participants are aware of the risk management plan, and it is tested periodically (twice a year) to ensure it executes if it has not been needed previously.	A risk issue evolves and the plan does not execute, or the plan is tested and aspects of the plan fail.	Ministry leaders have a mandatory call meeting with participants to review issues affecting adherence to this objective. Actions are put into place to regain control.

Fellowship activities (Trey)	Fellowship activities are identified in advance and added to the calendar quarterly as agreed.	Ministry participants are aware of and consistently attend and achieve the expected objectives.	Less than 75% of the ministry attend or objectives are not consistently met.	Ministry leaders have a mandatory call meeting with participants to review issues affecting adherence to this objective. Actions are put into place to regain control.

Find a Model Ministry for Your Transformation

Leading change and transformation is often a challenge because those who are following cannot picture a future they have not yet seen. I encourage churches to send ministry leaders and participants on benchmarking excursions to inspire the change. Find a church that is consistently operating now as the future state toward which you are moving. This is a valuable practice for the music and worship arts ministry as well as others. Connect with the appropriate contacts to see if you can sit in on a rehearsal, attend services, and interview ministry leaders and participants. Understand the best practices that helped them transform, understand challenges and how they were addressed, and understand practices of the ministry that worked well.

In addition to best practices, ask questions about systems, software, training, and other resources leveraged to equip people for the ministry. Equipping paid and volunteer staff is important to the success of the ministry and is often an area that gets overlooked.

The Music and Worship Ministry Model of WOCC

To offer an example on how to approach this, I have interviewed Napoleon Graves, Pastor of Music Worship and Arts at World Overcomers Christian Church (WOCC) in Durham, North Carolina. He works full time in the ministry and oversees planning, preparation, and execution for two Sunday morning services at two locations and Wednesday night mid-week service at only the

Durham location. The core musical singing is delivered by the praise and worship team. There is one adult mixed voice choir that sings periodically. The youth church has its own praise and worship singers (Graves, 2017).

The senior pastor and first lady are Pastor Andy Thompson and Lady LaShawn Thompson. The couple relocated from Boston to Durham and officially launched WOCC in 2003 with a handful of members. Pastor Andy is a multi-talented visionary, author, and international faith leader whose teachings enable balanced victory in a God-designed life. Today there are over 10,000 members between two locations in the Raleigh-Durham area (World Overcomers Christian Church, 2017).

On our first visit in January 2015, my husband and I were immediately drawn to the excellence in presentation of the powerful music and worship ministry and the relevant word for everyday application. At the time, I was serving as music director at another church, yet found this to be a place where I could go and receive ministry without having to be on duty.

Pastor Napoleon Graves (2017) originated from Boston, Massachusetts, where he and his brothers were reared in a musical family with an early start in church programs. Their demonstrated talents soon landed them positions as church musicians—Napoleon was even a minister of music at age 15. As they grew older, they eventually became a part of the Boston local music scene that continues to be heavily populated and influenced by the exceptional talent attending Berklee College of Music. This exposed them to various genres of music that contributed to and shaped their musicianship.

Napoleon's ministry experience in Boston taught him how to understand the flow of worship and the selection of musical songs in a sequence. This ability would be a valuable skill set in the ministry he would help foster in North Carolina. Napoleon's brother Bruce Graves initially became associated with Pastor Andy Thompson as the drummer at his father's church in Boston. He connected Napoleon with Pastor Andy in 2003, when Pastor Andy was led to start his own ministry in Durham.

When Napoleon and his wife moved to Durham, the church had grown to approximately 250 members but didn't have a structured music ministry or musicians. By 2004, Napoleon, his brother Bruce, and other musicians were on board at World Overcomers, which had a praise and worship team instead of a choir. It was initially volunteer only with a mix of adult voices. He eventually launched a young adult praise team after meeting with candidates to explain the expectations. This demographic brought momentum to the music and worship ministry's growth.

Commitment Obtains and Sustains the Change

From the beginning of Napoleon's music ministry involvement, a key success factor was to instill the value of commitment early, even with volunteers. Some churches struggle to expect high levels of commitment from volunteers, yet using them is essential to moving the ministry forward. The young adult team practiced consistently five to six months before they were a part of the public worship at World Overcomers. This is similar to the expectation of the Levites. They were required to demonstrate commitment spiritually and musically before being approved for public ministry.

The Risk of Over-Commitment

Pastor Napoleon noted that volunteers often over commit themselves with good intentions, yet this prohibits the best output. As my research also revealed, the issue of over-commitment occurs when music ministry participants are involved in multiple choirs or church ministries. As a result, they split their availability at the expense of the others. For this reason, when Pastor Napoleon became the minister of music, he did not launch multiple music entities. WOCC operated only with a praise and worship team. As he put it, they focused on "keeping the main thing the main thing." Over -commitment does not allow the ministry to produce the level of presentation and excellence that should represent the kingdom of God. If your ministry does not have the resources and capabilities to effectively deliver excellence with multiple choirs, perhaps there is an issue of over-commitment. You may need to do more with less. Have one "main thing" or main choir or praise team, while the others sing less often, even if you only run this schedule part of the year. Quality of worship is more important than quantity of music groups in the church.

Purpose, Expectations, and Participation

Pastor Napoleon says it is important to develop a foundational understanding of purpose in praise and worship. When he first arrived at WOCC, he spent several months teaching this purpose and gaining a clear understanding among the participants of their role. This alignment in understanding is essential to development and to obtaining accountability. He teaches the singers that their role is to lead people into God's presence and to get them in right relationship with God so the Word can saturate their hearts.

Spiritual and musical requirements are a part of the expectations for participation. When Pastor Napoleon initially came to the church, the praise and worship ministry consisted of volunteers without a selection process. After teaching on purpose, they began to select those who were best fit for the purpose and could best meet the demands of the ministry.

The selection process was based on spiritual maturity, technical ability, availability, and knowledge of praise and worship. He was willing to sacrifice passion over "puffed-up" attitudes. He looked at their humility. The singers had to sing three songs. One song was from the song set at the church, one song of their choice, and a song to test their ability to pick up quickly and retain.

He conducted interviews to gain a deeper understanding of the candidate's likelihood of success in participating in a very demanding ministry. One of the questions asked in the interview was designed to gauge the candidate's understanding of his or her actual calling.

He also asked candidates if they would leave the church if they were not selected. Those who did not make it received feedback on what they needed to work on. Some returned at the next audition time, after applying the feedback, and were successful in their subsequent audition.

A handbook clearly documenting the expectations of all participants was implemented and continues to be provided today, 15 years later. The last page must be signed, acknowledging agreement and accountability. Whenever people fall outside the expectations, Pastor Napoleon reviews this documentation with the participant. When expectations are not being met, the handbook guidelines are enforced. Some people have voluntarily taken time away because of issues in their personal lives. The handbook is part of the process for sustaining control and operation in the transformed state.

Challenges Faced While Moving Forward

Growth brings growing pains and unforeseen challenges in the route to the future state. Pastor Napoleon shared that leading leaders is a challenge. Occasionally, there may be some who do not understand how to follow. They sometimes have to be reminded that great leaders were once great followers.

The growth forward at times brought wear and tear on volunteers. Sometimes the music ministry entrance process was shortened because they needed singers. Taking the short-cut was later realized to be a detriment to the music ministry. From this experience, the key take-away is that it is important to carefully weigh the risk of critical decisions in the way forward.

Sometimes people lost morale and lost sight of the purpose along the path forward. They brought the wrong attitude and spirit during the worship service. This spirit attached to their gift, and this is what they delivered to the congregation. From this circumstance, the key take-away is that when we are not prepared spiritually or even technically to lead the worship experience, the congregation we are leading and whose hearts we are preparing suffers the consequence.

The ministry participants need to be constantly reminded of the purpose and vision to prevent distractions and drifting off the path.

The Vision Is the New Normal and New Reality

Pastor Napoleon is now operating music and worship of WOCC in the vision pursued in 2003. Planning growth continues, and goal setting does not stop. A debut CD entitled *The Sound* is currently available at online music market places. A sophomore CD release entitled *More* is planned for 2018 with tour dates to promote the CD. He spends time now on sustaining the excellence and monitoring the "new normal." It took approximately one year from 2003 to cultivate and obtain the vision for the music and worship ministry. As WOCC continues to grow, he has to make necessary adjustments to meet the demands of church growth. A second campus in Raleigh was launched in 2015, and Pastor Napoleon has replicated his processes to operate music and worship at the Raleigh campus.

Sustaining Quality of Excellence in Worship

The worship experience at WOCC consistently delivers a quality of excellence in presentation, production, and effectiveness. We need this to persevere the challenges we face in today's world and to overcome the difficulties of our personal lives.

I asked Pastor Napoleon to share what has worked best in sustaining quality of excellence in worship at WOCC. The readiness and preparation are rigorous. Once someone is selected as a singer, he or she must attend nine consecutive rehearsals without missing any. They must be able to demonstrate that they can practice independently, and that they are prepared to rehearse with others. They have to show that they can learn the WOCC modifications to current gospel releases and that they can follow the spiritually-led flow. This is demonstrated before they are approved to sing publicly to the congregation.

It takes highly skilled and committed individuals to accomplish the week-to-week worship service demands. Worship leaders submit songs for approval to Pastor Napoleon one week in advance. He then compiles a set of songs that is practiced on Mondays. The band and singers first rehearse separately for a couple of hours, and by the end of the evening, they all rehearse together. Worship leaders teach vocal parts to the worship teams while Pastor Napoleon practices with the musicians. By the upcoming Sunday, the band and singers are ready to deliver the set of songs.

Pastor Napoleon uses *PlanningCenterOnline.com* as software to help manage the music and worship ministry readiness and to communicate to singers and musicians. It provides structure to the planning process. It allows users to share playlists, enabling participants to practice at home and to be prepared to rehearse at rehearsal, rather than learning the material at rehearsal. Learning is done privately.

In addition to the week-to-week activities, Pastor Napoleon sets quarterly goals for the music ministry. He meets every two weeks with his worship leaders for strategic discussions regarding current goal status. Some goals have been missed, or they have taken some risk only to later overachieve the set goal.

Training and Preparing Your Leadership

Pastor Napoleon's leadership of the growth in music and worship at WOCC consists of trial, error, and adjustment, applying practices he learned from other ministries, looking for techniques outside the four walls of the church, and attending music conferences. The most impactful conference to his growth as a leader was held at Saddleback Church where Rick Warren is the senior pastor. Warren is the author of best-selling books *Purpose Driven Church* and *Purpose Driven Life.*

Additionally, it was helpful for Pastor Napoleon to have a full-time position as the music and worship arts pastor when he came to WOCC in 2003. This has allowed him to make a full commitment without distractions from another job. There was a growth process for the ministry budget-wise to be able to support the music and arts development, but it has proven to be a benefit to the growth of the church. Pastor Andy empowered Napoleon to lead the ministry and has given him the space and support to allow it to manifest.

Advice to Smaller Churches (300 Members or Less)

In summary, I asked Pastor Napoleon what advice he could offer smaller churches that face challenges in achieving and sustaining excellence in their music and worship arts ministry.

- Implement the expectation and vision up front.
- Have policies and procedures to keep participants accountable.
- While a small church, take sufficient time to focus on training and developing in areas that need strengthening.
- Many churches struggle with the idea of selecting participants. You owe it to those to whom you minister to be presented with your best and most prepared abilities.
- Improve the production level in the church in order to present the best abilities in your church.
  Your competition is the world and not the next church. The music presented in the church needs to be better than the world and the experience available in the world (club, radio, TV, Internet, etc).
- Your participants need to broaden their playlist and listen to more genres to grow musical abilities and technical exposure.
- Examine your demographics and make sure your resources are sufficient to grow choirs and praise and worship. Be efficient and do more with less.

Personal Self-Control in Our Future State

To sustain the improvements in our transformed music and worship arts ministry, we will need to work on our own self-control. Consistent prayer and study for the ministry will be needed to sustain the transform. We cannot expect the ministry to consistently operate within the control plan if individually we are not expecting ourselves to be spiritually disciplined and controlled. We must be individually renewed and transformed if we expect our ministry output to be renewed and transformed (Arnold-McFarland A. M., 2015–2017).

Personal Testimonies

There are personal benefits of a life of self-control. Our spiritual self-control is evidence of spiritual maturity and the way we allow our faith to work in all areas of our lives. Our daily walk is to live in the world but not be of the world. To walk by faith and not by sight. We are tempted to lean to our own understanding in our struggles and to not allow room for God to be God. Why do we do this? Because we try to understand God through the eyes we see with and the brain we reason with and through all of our normal channels of processing the world around us. His thoughts and abilities transcend what we can imagine. Remaining girded in our faith to be "in tune" with this requires self-control.

In my own life, I can personally testify to discernments or foresights of events that I cannot reason or understand. As one example, in 2013, I went to the doctor for a pain in my leg, which he thought was a pulled muscle since I was not at any medical risk for blood clots. The discerning Spirit of the Lord guided me to the right resources and contacts to be sure of the reason for this pain, even after my doctor had already told me it was not a blood clot and refused to see me again for a few days. I have doctors in the family who encouraged me to seek a diagnostic test, although the likelihood of a blood clot was low. It was by the grace of God that I found an urgent care facility that would provide a doppler ultrasound of my left leg. They sent me to radiology center that was about to close for the day but decided to wait for me to drive over. To my surprise, there was a blood clot in my leg. That night I was put on a blood thinner that would begin working on the clot right away. I was not hospitalized and went to choir rehearsal to direct and live normally. It was painful, yet I was thankful for the grace of God and the discerning spirit. This was a daily walk of faith to live with a clot for nine months. The next day I called the doctor who had misdiagnosed me and shortly afterward changed primary care doctors after 15 years. There was always the thought of the clot breaking away causing more harm or even death. Yet I had to walk by faith and not by the sight of my swollen leg or by the sight of reminders in the world of those who had blood clots and did not live through them.

Even more recently, in summer 2016, I began having dizzy and light-headed flashes on and off that happened daily at times, throughout the day, until spring 2017. My new doctor (whom I highly recommend) involved specialists, who were not able to diagnose the cause after running a series of tests. One day after service, I mentioned this to Minister Bruce Graves, the drummer for the worship band and one of the ministers at World Overcomers. He immediately prayed for me in the lobby. After about a month, this issue had diminished considerably. I informed my doctor of the change, and he continued to monitor it. I recall a conversation sometime after this with a ministry colleague who told me he had experienced an illness that had hospitalized him but overcame the problem after commanding his body to behave. I chose to do the same thing and spoke this, prayed and recalled the faith connection I had in the lobby at church, as well as continuously putting my heart into the presence of God in corporate and private worship. The problem diminished and eventually disappeared. My doctor has asked me to explain what I did differently. The only thing I did physically was gain some unwanted pounds (smile). The other things I did were spiritual: prayer and continued praise and worship. I know there is power in prayer, and continued worship admonishes me to stay faithful. The world tells us to pray and still doubt, or don't even bother to pray. The Word tells us to pray without doubt. It takes discipline and self-control to trust God. Let Him in your life, even in areas where you are afraid to trust Him. Once God has moved mountains and amazed you, your worship intensity will go to a higher level. Our worship experiences at church should refuel us and position us spiritually for healing, breakthroughs, and access to victorious living through Jesus Christ.

Rely on these study scriptures to grow toward self-control.

> I beseech you therefore, brethren, by the mercies of God, that you present your bodies a living sacrifice, holy, acceptable to God, *which is* your reasonable service. And do not be conformed to this world, but be transformed by the renewing of your mind, that you may prove what *is* that good and acceptable and perfect will of God.
>
> Romans 12:1–2

> But also for this very reason, giving all diligence, add to your faith virtue, to virtue knowledge, to knowledge self-control, to self-control perseverance, to perseverance godliness, to godliness brotherly kindness, and to brotherly kindness love. For if these things are yours and abound, *you* will be neither barren nor unfruitful in the knowledge of our Lord Jesus Christ.
>
> 2 Peter 1:5–8

> Better *to be* of a humble spirit with the lowly, than to divide the spoil with the proud.
>
> Proverbs 16:19

> Now the fruit of righteousness is sown in peace by those who make peace.
>
> James 3:18

> But the fruit of the Spirit is love, joy, peace, longsuffering, kindness, goodness, faithfulness, gentleness, and self-control. Against such there is no law.
>
> Galatians 5:22–23

> I desire therefore that the men pray everywhere, lifting up holy hands, without wrath and doubting.
>
> 1 Timothy 2:8

Interactive Learning Activity:

What self-discipline and control do you need to sustain to be fit spiritually, mentally, and physically for purpose in the music and worship arts ministry?

Add this to the growth you will achieve in your personal improvement plan.

Reference

Arnold-McFarland, A. M. (2015- 2017). Gospel Music One Sound Project.

Graves, N. (2017, Dec). The music and worship arts growth at World Overcomers Christian Church. (A. M. Arnold-McFarland, Interviewer)

About. (2017). *World Overcomers Christian Church.* Retrieved from https://www.worldovercomers.church/

CONCLUSION

It is my hope that this book compels pastors and music and worship arts ministry leaders to move forward and face the future, despite challenges faced in operating and executing ministry. My intent is to offer my services and solutions to aid in this critical charge to those who are called according to His purpose. Our world is facing perilous times, and we cannot afford to be less than our best as we face the tribulations of today. True worshipers who are skilled and equipped are needed to encourage believers in their faith, to help us use prayer and praise as a weapon that can ambush evil, to bring unity where there is division, to bring love where there is hatred, to heal where there is suffering, to be humanitarians where there is a need, to bring peace during tribulation, and to win over souls lost by the ways of the world.

For 400 years, African-Americans and the Black Church have demonstrated how the songs of our faith can pull people through horrors, social injustices, inequalities, and assassinations. In June 2015, President Obama "raised" the hymn (as it is commonly called in the Black Church) *Amazing Grace.* He eulogized state Senator Rev. Clementa Pickney and memorialized all nine victims killed by a racially motivated shooter after Bible study at Emmanuel A.M.E. in Charleston, South Carolina. This song soothed the aching soul of America as others attending the service joined in and were moved by the singing. President Obama stated that if we can find that grace, anything is possible, and if we can tap into that grace, everything can change. We later saw how the families of the victims demonstrated amazing grace as they offered the shooter forgiveness as Christ has forgiven us. Does your worship experience equip lives to face a horror such as this, yielding forgiveness to the murderer of your loved ones? This act of forgiveness is a sacrificial worship that speaks volumes about the pastoring of Rev. Pickney. This is worship in spirit and truth at its best.

We later saw the removal of the Confederate flag from the state capital of South Carolina. There was a long-lived battle in this, my home state, where my family was regularly victimized by racially motivated vandalism and senseless tactics. I also saw two KKK marches in my life while growing up there and the use of this flag for white supremacist rallies. There is deep-rooted connection to the Confederate flag in South Carolina, as it was the first state to pull out of the Union. Many who once were blind to the hatred and bigotry this flag fosters have come to see the reality as they mourn the lost lives of people who did not deserve to die like this. This later led a movement across the nation to remove Confederate memorials that motivate racist terrorism and hatred against all people. Worship in church, not just the Black Church, touched the hearts of lawmakers in South Carolina to agree to a bi-partisan initiative to "move us forward" to face the future better than the now. As shown here, the evidence of worship is a transformation that moves us closer to the heart of Christ. This is just one example, but we continue to see church shootings, school shootings, and other public mass shootings that need the results of our worship to compel lawmakers and others who can influence change. We must be social change agents of faith like Dr. King and others whose worship helped transform the moral compass and integrity of society.

Our plantation field songs moved us forward from slavery to the Jim Crow Era, and our devotional songs moved us forward from Jim Crow to the Civil Rights Era. Our hymns and freedom songs moved us from the Civil Rights Era to black liberation. Our soul stirring gospel music has moved us from black liberation to black lives matter. We need all these songs to move us forward from black lives matter to *all* lives matter as we face a future of horrific mass shootings, natural disasters, terrorism, and the threat of nuclear war as nations rise against nations. The call to the music and worship arts ministry is to lead the worship experience in song, preparing the hearts of the people for a transformational word from the pastor and from those who disciple the teachings of Christ. We need people of all races, ethnicities, and walks of life to experience worship in such a way that they are compelled to behave, speak up, and change hearts and minds in such a way that they and lives around them are transformed. Our worship needs to be able to transcend differences, and even religions, so that it changes the world and makes it a place where people of differences can co-exist peacefully without oppression, discrimination, hatred, or bigotry. Our human nature to help our fellow mankind rules over inferiority. It is urgent that we move forward and face our future with true worshipers who have hope, who are prayerful, and who are better prepared to change the outlook.

Study Scriptures for Those Called According to His Purpose

> "But the hour is coming, and now is, when the true worshipers will worship the Father in spirit and truth; for the Father is seeking such to worship Him. God *is* Spirit, and those who worship Him must worship in spirit and truth."
>
> John 4:23–24

> Rejoicing in hope, patient in tribulation, continuing steadfastly in prayer."
>
> Romans 12:12

> Now when they began to sing and to praise, the LORD set ambushes against the people of Ammon, Moab, and Mount Seir, who had come against Judah; and they were defeated.
>
> 2 Chronicles 20:22

But know this, that in the last days perilous times will come: For men will be lovers of themselves, lovers of money, boasters, proud, blasphemers, disobedient to parents, unthankful, unholy, unloving, unforgiving, slanderers, without self-control, brutal, despisers of good, traitors, headstrong, haughty, lovers of pleasure rather than lovers of God, having a form of godliness but denying its power. And from such people turn away!

2 Timothy 3:2–5

For the time will come when they will not endure sound doctrine, but according to their own desires, *because* they have itching ears, they will heap up for themselves teachers; and they will turn *their* ears away from the truth, and be turned aside to fables. But you be watchful in all things, endure afflictions, do the work of an evangelist, fulfill your ministry.

2 Timothy 4:3–4

"For nation will rise against nation, and kingdom against kingdom. And there will be famines, pestilences, and earthquakes in various places."

Matthew 24:7

"And there will be signs in the sun, in the moon, and in the stars; and on the earth distress of nations, with perplexity, the sea and the waves roaring."

Luke 21:25

"And there will be great earthquakes in various places, and famines and pestilences; and there will be fearful sights and great signs from heaven."

Luke 21:11

"And it shall come to pass in that day," says the Lord GOD, "That I will make the sun go down at noon, And I will darken the earth in broad daylight."

Amos 8:9

And we know that all things work together for good to those who love God, to those who are the called according to *His* purpose.

Romans 8:28

"When I shut up heaven and there is no rain, or command the locusts to devour the land, or send pestilence among My people, if My people who are called by My name will humble themselves, and pray and seek My face, and turn from their wicked ways, then I will hear from heaven, and will forgive their sin and heal their land."

2 Chronicles 7:13–14

APPENDICES

APPENDIX ONE

Quick Reference Guide for Practical Solutions

This quick reference solutions guide has been compiled from categorizing a host of issues and frequently asked questions (FAQs) identified in the Gospel Music One Sound Project research. This data driven research conducted on smaller budget African-American churches has revealed similarities in issues as outlined previously in this book. The focus area summarizes the types of issues and FAQs in the specific category. Review the recommended practice and actions associated with the issues and FAQs. Reference other books and Scripture for further understanding on each subtopic. Move forward girded with the Word of truth. If your church has a new issue that is not listed in this book, please contact me so I can include emerging issues in my ongoing research and subsequent publications.

<table>
<tr><td colspan="2">Focus Areas
Organizational Leadership and Alignment/Budgeting/ Vision, Strategic Planning and Execution/Inspiration for Change</td></tr>
<tr><td>Top Issues From Survey and FAQs</td><td>Recommended Practices and Actions</td></tr>
<tr><td>The pastor and leadership lack awareness of the relevant strategies for effective music ministry.

What makes a music ministry effective and what steps need to occur to achieve this?

How do you plan a vision for the music ministry?</td><td>Leadership, strategy and vision: These issues and questions come from the lack of a strategic plan for growth and a ministry vision. The vision is the foundation that links the participants to a plan of operation in the present and transformed state for the future. The music and worship arts ministry vision, direction, and strategy should align with the direction and vision set by leadership for the church.

The SWOT Analysis can be used to diagnose and set strategies. Small projects and initiatives can be launched to resolve issues identified from the SWOT. As demonstrated in this book, intentional strategy and improvement actions move the ministry forward to effectiveness. A music ministry consultant can help arrive at goals and an improvement plan.

Refer to Steven Ford's book, Is your Music Department Ministry or Misery? This is a practical guide for the pastor and music ministry leadership

Scriptures to study:

"Then the LORD answered me and said: 'Write the vision and make it plain on tablets that he may run who reads it. For the vision is yet for an appointed time; but at the end it will speak, and it will not lie. Though it tarries, wait for it; Because it will surely come, it will not tarry.'"
Habakkuk 2:2–3

"Where there is no revelation, people cast off restraint; but blessed is the one who heeds wisdom's instruction."
Proverbs 29:18 NIV

"Moreover you shall select from all the people able men, such as fear God, men of truth, hating covetousness; and place such over them to be rulers of thousands, rulers of hundreds, rulers of fifties, and rulers of tens."
Exodus 18:21

"Be diligent to know the state of your flocks, and attend to your herds; For riches are not forever, nor does a crown endure to all generations."
Proverbs 27:23–24

"Do you see a man who excels in his work? He will stand before kings; He will not stand before unknown men."
Proverbs 22:29</td></tr>
</table>

The budget does not retain the right skill sets for the music ministry The budget does not include education and seminars for choir members Why do churches delay building their music department and setting an appropriate budget?	**Budgeting:** The music and worship arts ministry budget does not retain the right skills and does not include further training when there is a lack of knowledge by leadership as to what is required to grow the ministry. As a result, there is a delay in response to the need to appropriately set the budget. This is often the case in smaller churches. Focus on what is affordable in the short term until more consistent funding is available. Incorporate training by sending a few representatives to training who can come back and transfer the knowledge. Or co-host a training seminar with other churches to share the cost. To retain good talent, have a musician on some Sundays but not all Sundays. Pay the same amount monthly, but focus on a few Sundays with more impact. Here are some other alternatives to cover service music without a musician: use tracks instead of live music, have singers who effectively sing acapella, or intentionally incorporate some congregational singing without instruments. Use your funds/resources selectively and efficiently. There is a cost to doing ministry, so it is important to have clearly defined and written roles/responsibilities for paid staff and for volunteers. **For salary information reference** *The African-American Church Musician's Compensation and Salary Handbook* by R.W. Perry II. Sold by ntimemusic.om **Scriptures to study:** "Now to him who works, the wages are not counted as grace but as debt." Romans 4:4 "But this *I say:* He who sows sparingly will also reap sparingly, and he who sows bountifully will also reap bountifully." 2 Corinthians 9:6

How do you generate change in the culture and traditions of the church choir? How do you establish an effective choir in a small congregation? How do you move forward when there is limited time for preparation, (1–2 rehearsals per week), part-time staff, increasing demands to improve and grow repertoire, and a lack of demonstrated interest from the choir to meet the demands?	**Inspiring change:** Change starts with the church leadership agreeing and empowering the music ministry leadership to make changes for the best. Choir members and others in worship and arts ministry need spiritual nurturing to accept change. This is obtained by devoted study of scriptures on music and worship arts and the music ministry modeled by the Levites and on commitment. Schedule time to study and gird the ministry with biblical foundations of music, worship, and spiritual growth. Music seminars provide growth, relevancy, and continuous improvement. Ongoing training should be required of at least the music ministry staff and officers. Vocal and technical skills can be improved once there is a mind-set for transformation. Small churches have fewer resources, yet training is still accessible where sought and it is required to represent God and to give Him your best. Quality of singers is more impactful than quantity of singers. Select music that fits the capabilities of the choir and musicians and deliver it with excellence. The ministry's demands cannot exceed your capacity of talent, funding, and time. Quality music and worship arts output is produced within the consistent capabilities of your operation. If you want more output, the leadership and ministry must be willing to invest more input. Feelings of anxiety on meeting the demands of the ministry can be relieved by revisiting the vision and setting a reasonable strategy and plan for improvement. The quality of music is more impactful than the quantity of music. **Scriptures to study:** "But this *I say:* He who sows sparingly will also reap sparingly, and he who sows bountifully will also reap bountifully." 2 Corinthians 9:16 "Create in me a clean heart, O God, And renew a steadfast spirit within me." Psalm 51:10 "I will give you a new heart and put a new spirit within you; I will take the heart of stone out of your flesh and give you a heart of flesh." Ezekiel 36:26 "And do not be conformed to this world, but be transformed by the renewing of your mind, that you may prove what *is* that good and acceptable and perfect will of God." Romans 12:2 "'For I know the plans I have for you,' declares the LORD, 'plans to prosper you and not to harm you, plans to give you hope and a future.'" Jeremiah 29:11 NIV (For everything that was written in the past was written to teach us, so that through the endurance taught in the Scriptures and the encouragement they provide we might have hope." Romans 15:4 NIV

<table>
<tr><td colspan="2">Focus Areas
Commitment and Engagement</td></tr>
<tr><th>Top Issues From Survey and FAQs</th><th>Recommended Practices and Actions</th></tr>
<tr><td>How do you increase consistency in participation?

How do you get more church members to participate in all aspects of the music ministry?

How can a choir director increase morale in the choir when the minister of music does not have passion and enthusiasm for the calling?</td><td>Commitment: An increase in consistent participation must be preceded by an increase in understanding of calling and purpose. This occurs through study and knowledge of the applicable scriptures on music, worship, and spiritual growth. See vision and strategic planning sub-topic.

Engagement: Choir member recruitment should come through an invitation and a selective entry process that considers spiritual readiness, a teachable spirit, and vocal potential. The talent search for potential candidates can start with a music ministry "open house" to interview and have one-on-one conversations with those interested. Another option is to have Sundays when interested parties can "try out" the choir before they commit. Perhaps this is a fifth Sunday choir or seasonal choir. Potential candidates can also attend rehearsal to observe before they decide to move further.

The music ministry leadership must realize that their level of passion transmits to those under their influence. The lack of passion could mean there is a need for exposure to a conference, seminar, or other activity for repurposing and rejuvenation. A sabbatical is often needed to allow time for refreshing, even if it means a leave without pay. As leaders in ministry, we must realize that our timeframe for impact has a start and end time. When one season ends, another one begins with a new assignment.

Choir members can be motivated and inspired by attending training or major national conference. If this is not possible, host an event locally and invite a guest clinician to revive the calling. Regular fellowship activity is a way to maintain motivation, passion, and engagement. See Influencing Change subtopic. See Chapter One on understanding worship. The purpose of the music ministry is to lead public and corporate worship.

Scriptures to study:

"Therefore comfort each other and edify one another, just as you also are doing."
1 Thessalonians 5:11

"Let the word of Christ dwell in you richly in all wisdom, teaching and admonishing one another in psalms and hymns and spiritual songs, singing with grace in your hearts to the Lord."
Colossians 3:16</td></tr>
</table>

<table>
<tr><td>What qualities are demonstrated by an effective choir?</td><td>Gospel Music One Sound Project Webinar with Professor L. Stanley Davis (Nov 2015)

• Vocal preparation and voice care is demonstrated.
• Vocalists are able to sing a basic tune.
• The choir demonstrates commitment and dedication.
• There is willingness to rehearse several hours per week at a minimum.
• Vocalists practice privately outside of rehearsal.
• Vocal warm-ups occur in the first 30 minutes.
• Vocalists have a relationship with Christ that is apparent.
• There is a commitment to serve the congregation.
• Lyrics are articulated and understood by the audience.</td></tr>
<tr><td>What is needed for effectiveness today in music ministry and for those aspiring to reach goals in the gospel music industry?</td><td>• Local church, community, and the aspiring gospel artist/group

o Commitment and dedication to the ministry and the message
o A continued desire to be teachable
o A plan and execution of activities for learning (short term and long term)
o Spiritual connection to the audience (music that compels, convicts, converts, changes)
o Demonstrated technical capability, presentation, and clear message
o Resources (time, funding, facilities, equipment, etc.)
o Support team and resources who believe in your ministry, vision and will grow with it
o Business savviness, professionalism, and follow through (for church and industry)
o Creativity, innovation, and relevance
o Prayer life and perseverance</td></tr>
</table>

<table>
<tr><td colspan="2">Focus Areas
Effectiveness of Equipment: Instruments, Audio, Sound, and Media</td></tr>
<tr><td>Top Issues From Survey and FAQs</td><td>Recommended Practices and Actions</td></tr>
<tr><td>How do you get a good mix of sound that balances music level with vocals?</td><td>Sound, audio, and projection media are the worship arts skill sets that often get overlooked. These areas enable music delivery and the worship experience. Musicians, vocalists, and audio and media techs must all work in one accord for God's glory and not for self.

Sound and audio: Everyone who uses the audio and sound equipment needs, at a minimum, a basic understanding of how to use the equipment so a qualified sound technician can make adjustments to deliver live quality output. For example, you should test the microphone by speaking or singing into it, not by beating it with your hands. This is damaging to electronic equipment. Use it the way you will use for the live performance. If you will not be beating the microphone in the song, then there is no need to beat it to test it.

Diagnosing audio and sound mix issues includes reviewing the impact of these main factors: the design of the worship space or sanctuary, the positioning of the speakers and monitors, the specifications of the equipment in this space, and the capabilities of the singers and musicians. There can also be a lack of critical equipment to support the sound production. The qualified sound technician makes the necessary adjustment to each sound input from instruments and vocals to get the best output, considering all these factors. Start with the band—drums first—balancing the bass guitar to the bass drums. Then balance the lead guitar and keys. Once the music mix is good, bring in the choir, then the lead vocals.

The mix can be diagnosed and improved by doing a good sound check before the service. The sound and audio techs should attend the choir rehearsal to effectively prepare for the upcoming service.

Sound and Audio Training: The audio and sound ministry needs trained technicians who can demonstrate their abilities. If there is no one in your congregation qualified to determine this, find a resource outside the church to assist in training and in assessing abilities. Keep in mind that the gifts and talent in sound and audio may be among people who work in music venues beyond church music. They operate sound boards for paid events, like concerts and productions, and deliver their skill sets accordingly for their profession. Volunteers must be willing to put in sufficient time to deliver professionally.

Reference: There are online resources and forums in this area. Visit churchmix.com and search YouTube videos on church sound and audio.

Scriptures to study:

"Study to shew thyself approved unto God, a workman that needeth not to be ashamed, rightly dividing the word of truth."
2 Timothy 2:15 KJV

"Let nothing be done through selfish ambition or conceit, but in lowliness of mind let each esteem others better than himself. [4] Let each of you look out not only for his own interests, but also for the interests of others."
Philippians 2:3–4</td></tr>
</table>

Musicians do not understand how to accompany the singers at a volume level that does not overpower the vocals. Choir members do not project and sing with confidence, thus making it hard for musicians to accompany them.	**Instruments:** Defining volume as "too loud" or "too soft" is relative to the listener or to the individual producing the sound. From the perspective of the listener, if the volume is too loud, here are a few common reasons: singers or musicians are overcompensating to hear themselves against other sound produced at the same time; they are not close enough to the speaker or monitor to hear themselves; or they need to work on their skill sets in understanding orchestration, harmony, and control. Sometimes our emotions tempt us to lose control of the delivery. Musicians and singers must keep in mind that they must make adjustments to have "one sound" and the chemistry to produce the best output for a spirit-filled worship experience. In the Black Church, playing and singing by ear and without sheet music is the norm. Our ears are like our "eyes." We use our ears to give us insight to where the song is going. Insufficient hearing is like using a GPS that gives you directions too late. You miss turns because of unclear directions. A good sound check helps you realize audio challenges prior to the service. When this does not execute right during service, go back and troubleshoot to figure out what went wrong so the problem does not repeat itself. **Scriptures to study:** "And the Levites *who were* the singers, all those of Asaph and Heman and Jeduthun, with their sons and their brethren, stood at the east end of the altar, clothed in white linen, having cymbals, stringed instruments and harps, and with them one hundred and twenty priests sounding with trumpets—indeed it came to pass, when the trumpeters and singers *were* as one, to make one sound to be heard in praising and thanking the LORD, and when they lifted up their voice with the trumpets and cymbals and instruments of music, and praised the LORD, *saying: 'For He is* good, For His mercy *endures* forever' that the house, the house of the LORD, was filled with a cloud, so that the priests could not continue ministering because of the cloud; for the glory of the LORD filled the house of God." 2 Chronicles 5:12–14
Lyrics projected lag behind the worship leader.	**Media:** Projecting lyrics on the screen is one way to increase participation of the congregation. It's not necessary, but it is helpful in increasing participation in singing. Those who project lyrics need to attend rehearsal and get coordinated with the flow of the song and style of the worship leader. They must understand that in the Black Church, our custom and culture is often to improvise the song. It may not go exactly as rehearsed. They must be comfortable in supporting this.

How does a church improve their quality of sound at a reasonable and affordable price?	**Budgeting for sound equipment**: Find several similarly sized churches with a good sound, audio, and projection ministry. Ask them to share the type of equipment purchased, the budget set, and the name of the company or consultant they used. Understand what went well for their experience and what did not go as well, so you do not repeat their mistakes. Gently used equipment is a good option if you can find trustworthy sources that sell it. The equipment can be obtained over time, starting with the most critical components first. Plan a budget based on this research, plan for growth, and work toward training technicians, musicians, and vocalists. Assign someone to lead this effort with a set timeline to have it in place.

Focus Areas Spiritual Maturity	
Top Issues From Survey and FAQs	**Recommended Practices and Actions**
What do you do when the choir has grown stagnant and is not growing spiritually? How do you handle friction, jealousy and animosity among choir members?	Spiritual maturity issues exist today because the choir is volunteer in most black churches and does not require demonstration of spiritual maturity as a qualification. Many choir members and musicians lack an understanding of their role and responsibility to the music and worship ministry. A good Bible study on the requirements of choir members technically and spiritually addresses spiritual immaturity. Participants in all ministries, not just music, need to have consistent spiritual growth. Without this, there will always be carnal-minded conflicts like jealously, division, pride, and unhealthy competition. The music and worship arts ministry is not a place for people to be served. It is a place for people who want to serve the congregation. **Scripture to study:** *"Let* nothing *be done* through selfish ambition or conceit, but in lowliness of mind let each esteem others better than himself. Let each of you look out not only for his own interests, but also for the interests of others." Philippians 2:3–4 (in effectiveness of equipment) Refer to and review the causes of worship challenges. There is too much to add on this topic to fit in this space. Also read Steven Ford's book, *Is Your Music Department Ministry or Misery?*

Focus Areas Awareness, Preparation, Training, and Repertoire	
Top Issues From Survey and FAQs	**Recommended Practices and Actions**
Choir members do not value exposure to vocal development and training seminars outside of rehearsal time. Choir members do not practice outside of rehearsal. Choir members lack consistency in participation, making it difficult to progress and learn new songs. How do you make our praise team more effective? How do you convince the music ministry the importance of teaching and learning songs well in advance, so the singers can fully grasp them and deliver them with total freedom, confidence, and excellence? How can you encourage choir members to rehearse outside of church?	**Awareness**: All music and worship arts ministry participants must be aware of the expectations of skill and delivery for singers and musicians modeled in Scripture by the Levites. Studying these gives them awareness and accountability to protocol, roles, and responsibilities. Singing in the music ministry has spiritual and technical requirements. The praise team should represent the model for the choir members to follow. They need this awareness in order to be more effective spiritually. If participants are not held accountable and are not willing to submit to music ministry expectations aligned with Scripture, then you cannot expect an outcome of excellence. Spiritual commitment, technical preparation, and a teachable spirit create the foundation for success. Participants must be willing to accept correction, to follow instructions, and to accept decisions that do not satisfy personal agendas and desires. They should want what is best for the ministry. There should be an entry and selection process for participation in the music and worship arts ministry. This would minimize the challenges in this focus area. They should be willing to prepare appropriately and willing to attend training to grow and develop before they are allowed to participate in the choir. Put guidelines in place for the expectations, and follow through on discipline for the benefit of the ministry. All this applies to the praise team as well, yet with higher expectations. **References:** Refer to the spiritual maturity focus area and Chapter Three. *The Choir Member's Companion* by Ginger Wyrick. **Scriptures to study:** Here are a few reference scriptures from Donnie McClurkin's 2011 Perfecting Music Conference held in Charlotte, NC: 1 Chronicles 15:22, 2 Chronicles 5:12–14, Psalm 100:1–2, Colossians 3:16. They outline guidelines and expectations for participants (singers, directors, worship leaders, instrumentalists). Whenever the spirit from God came on Saul, David would take up his lyre and play. Then relief would come to Saul; he would feel better, and the evil spirit would leave him. (See 1 Samuel 16:23 NIV.) Kenaniah the head Levite was in charge of the singing; that was his responsibility because he was skillful at it. (See 1 Chronicles 15:22 NIV.) 2 Chronicles 5:12–14 (NKVJ)

<table>
<tr><td></td><td>See Effectiveness of Equipment Focus Area key scriptures.

"Make a joyful shout to the Lord, all you lands! Serve the Lord with gladness; Come before His presence with singing."
Psalm 100:1–2

"Let the word of Christ dwell in you richly in all wisdom, teaching and admonishing one another in psalms and hymns and spiritual songs, singing with grace in your hearts to the Lord."
Colossians 3:16</td></tr>
<tr><td>How do you get the choir to record their parts and study their music?

What does private practice at home entail?

How often should you conduct choir/ music workshops?

What do you do when your musicians do not participate in the workshops?

Choir members participate in various other ministries, causing overlapping commitments.</td><td>Preparation and training: The minister of music should set basic technical requirements for participation. The Choir Member's Companion by Ginger Wyrick is a good handbook for decorum expectations and technical basics.

Private practice/preparation: The goal of all singers is to practice enough privately to accurately learn lyrics, sing their vocal part on pitch, and learn the arrangement of the song. At a minimum, this requires several times per week.

If singers are not naturally musically inclined, practicing each phrase by repetition until it can be sung independently is the best method for retaining parts on pitch. Some choir members may need to consider private lessons to meet these basic requirements.

Choir members can leverage technology like smart phones to record rehearsals. Or the vocal parts and a tutorial can be recorded and placed on a YouTube channel to provide a template for studying. They can watch it and listen via their phones, computers, and other electronic devices.

If choir members do not know how to use their phones in this manner, have a training session to increase technology skill sets with devices and computers. This will enable preparation outside of rehearsal.

Workshops/Seminars: Many choirs have workshops to learn new material and focus on choir decorum. The most important focus should be on biblical foundations. Have a seminar that studies the scriptures on music and worship before learning new songs. Everyone—musicians, singers, and audio and media participants—should have expectations to meet or exceed. If individuals refuse to participate, this is clear sign they do not have the right motivation for the ministry. This is a job fit and personnel issue. Ensure that the content covers their specific roles and responsibilities. This type of training should occur at least twice a year to inspire growth, sustain improvements, and align everyone toward the vision.</td></tr>
<tr><td></td><td>Preparation time constraints: Choir members are usually involved in other ministries. Over-commitment will affect available time to prepare. They should take a good look at how many hours are needed for their personal life and what they can commit to in each ministry. Failing to do this often affects consistency in participation. Lack of consistency hinders progress. An expectation of available hours needs to be set as a guideline.</td></tr>
</table>

How do you teach the praise team to select the appropriate songs for praise and worship? If a song is on the radio and the musician lowers the key, does this take away from the effectiveness of the song? Do you have the right balance of focus between the quality vs. quantity of songs that you perform? Why do people feel all hymns are for old saints and not the younger generation?	**Repertoire**: Increasing repertoire must be strategically planned with sufficient time to be effective. Quality of music and presentation prevails over quantity of music. Song selection for praise teams and choirs must match the capabilities of the choir. The most popular music on the radio is not necessarily the best fit for the choir. Find music through chorale books, new hymnal releases, music workshops, new songwriter releases, and other sources in addition to the radio. Ensure lyrics have the appropriate substance for the worship service. Every church needs to have a level of appreciation of hymns. They are based on Scripture. Hymns are for adoring and praising God—not for record sales. They are multi-generational just like the Word of God. All ages can appreciate them if the analysis of the lyrics is taught for better understanding. Other styles of Christian music emerged to accommodate ease of singing and the culture preferences and needs of daily living. This does not mean hymns should be neglected. They are harder to sing, and people tend to choose what is more culturally popular. The praise team should submit songs for approval to the minister of music or music director if the worship leader does not effectively select the right material. Songs should enhance participation of the congregation. The goal is to get to a place where all participants realize a need to worship with their own heart and their own lips. Adjusting the key maintains effectiveness if the delivery and presentation are still impactful. The vocalists should effectively use vocal mechanics and techniques and authenticity (believability) to get the best presentation of the song.

Focus Areas Personnel Issues/ Job fit/ Performance	
Top Issues From Survey and FAQs	**Recommended Practices and Actions**
What do you do when the minister of music has lost passion, does not want to learn new songs, does not want to improve the choir, and does not want to resign? How do you control strong personalities in the music ministry who have great demands without running them away?	**Personnel issues/job fit:** It is best to have guidelines and expectations in place for volunteer and paid personnel before a critical issue occurs. Regular feedback and performance evaluations should occur to prevent misalignments and misunderstandings and to allow time for adjustments if expectations are not being met. Ministry participants need to be aware of biblical foundations that set the spiritual and technical requirements of their role and responsibility. This is covered in the following focus areas: organizational leadership and alignment; spiritual maturity; and awareness, training, and preparation. Leaders are called to be good stewards over their contribution to ministry and have a role in accountability for how they oversee their assigned area of ministry. Music ministry participants must realize that leadership decisions are based on what is best for the overall progress of the music and worship arts ministry. These decisions may not necessarily satisfy personal desires and expectations. When people do not meet these standards and are provided time to improve and don't improve, then it is leadership's responsibilities to manage issues, even if it will be a difficult conversation. This might include dismissing people from their season in a specific ministry. Perhaps God is opening another door for them that they have not yet realized. **Scripture to study:** "For a bishop [overseer] must be blameless, as a steward of God, not self-willed, not quick-tempered, not given to wine, not violent, not greedy for money." Titus 1:7
How does one tactfully and without hurting self-esteem, explain to a choir member that his or her abilities are not a good fit for the music ministry?	**Performance:** Most church vocalists are not aware that the Levites were "red shirted" and had to be on the sidelines for an extended period of time before they were accepted for public worship. This is very much unlike what we do in ministry today. Since most choirs in the Black Church are volunteer and do not have an entry process, you will have worship challenges such as this. Some choir members need extra time beyond what is reasonably available to the music ministry leader. Suggest that they seek private lessons to be able to meet the basic expectations or offer them a "red-shirted" position until they can demonstrate they are ready. If they cannot do this or if it does not improve their performance, then suggest a support role to the choir or another ministry.

Should choir participation, whether vocal or instrumental, be contingent on participation in other aspects of church life, i.e., Bible study, Sunday school, or worship service, when they are not singing or playing, etc.?	Before a minister of music dismisses a choir member, it is best to discuss the issue with the senior pastor. Explain your reason for justifying the course of action and see if he/she agrees. Be sure to have facts on the reasonable options attempted before determining that dismissal is best for the music and worship arts ministry. If there is not agreement, then agree on the next best step. If there is agreement, find another ministry to suggest where the individual would be a better fit. Adapt this same course of action for other performance-based personnel issues. Pastors should discuss their decisions to dismiss the minister of music with fellow leadership and get facts from observing on their own. People's participation in the music ministry should include spiritual readiness and growth. This includes participation in activities such as Bible study, Sunday school, worship service, and training. Musicians and singers should not leave the worship service when the message is delivered. They should have an interest in hearing the preached Word. If they are leaving, this is a job performance issue. **Reference:** Chapter Three on Worship Challenges
How do you handle the challenges of being placed as the minister of music when the previous one was dismissed? Why is musician turnover rate high in some churches?	**Personnel transition**: When a new minister of music or music director comes to replace one that was dismissed, there will need to be time for emotional attachments to subside. At the same time, the incoming personnel must set standards and expectations. Teach new repertoire over time to allow the choir members to get used to the musical interpretation of the new music ministry leader. The pastor must be willing to support the change and cannot be influenced by choir members who circumvent the new music ministry leadership and complain to the pastor. It is best if the pastor first speaks to the choir about his/her expectation of the choir to support the transition and point complainers back to the new leadership before getting involved. Churches have high turnover rate if they if they are not careful to find a good fit for their ministry or if they do not know what they actually need for their ministry. What they want and what they have budgeted could misalign. There is a difference between a minister of music/music director and an accompanist. Everyone who plays the keyboard/organ is not the best fit for being a minister of music/music director. Be sure to examine the new candidate spiritually and start him or her on a probationary basis before making an offer. Some musicians are focused more on money and miss out on opportunities that would make even more room for their gift. At the same time, the church must be knowledgeable about what is considered reasonable and acceptable for talent. **Refer** to Steven Ford's book, *Is Your Music Department Ministry or Misery?* This is a practical guide for the pastor and music ministry leadership.

	For pay information and qualifications refer to *The African-American Church Musician's Compensation and Salary* Handbook by R.W. Perry II (sold on ntimemusic.com). **Scriptures to study:** "Whatever you do, work heartily, as for the Lord and not for men." Colossians 3:23 "A man's gift makes room for him, And brings him before great men." Proverbs 18:16

APPENDIX TWO

Moving Forward and Facing the Future; The Aspiring Gospel Artist of the Black Church Worship Experience

My doctoral research launched me into what I have named Gospel Music One Sound Project. This book has told only part of the story of how we face the future in the Black Church worship experience. The other portion must include the role of the gospel artists in the gospel music industry, a very influential entity in the Black Church worship experience. It is one of the three venues where African-American worship takes place: 1) the church 2) the community, and 3) the industry. I compiled best practices from secondary data in books, articles, and magazines, as well as from interviews and seminars with industry professionals. One particular event I attended was Donnie McClurkin's Perfecting Music Conference in 2011 in Charlotte, North Carolina. It was an opportunity to get first-hand counsel from those who used to be aspiring gospel artists (Perfecting Music Conference, 2011).

I am not sure if I will ever write another book to tell the rest of the story. In the event I don't, here are key take-away prescriptions from the research that can benefit aspiring gospel artists now. They have a unique set of challenges. My research was built around the problem of balancing ministry and industry.

The Problem of Balancing Ministry vs. Industry

The independent gospel artist is challenged to balance ministry against the demands of the music industry. As a disciple of Christ, the independent gospel artist is expected to spread the gospel through song, while not compromising or conforming to the conflicting values of the music industry aimed at mainstream cultural appeal. In other words, how does the independent gospel artist balance ministry focus against the demands of the industry and sustain effectiveness without compromising his or her Christian faith? (Arnold-McFarland A. M., 2016).

The answer lies in the research that traces the history and evolution of gospel music and in the various participants and factors that enable it. This approach arrives at best practices and trends of influential artists, industry professionals, and local church/community music ministry leaders in current times. When these elements are coupled with supportive changes in social acceptance, attitude, or perception, the environment for transformation and possibilities is fertilized. Thus, sustainable and effective improvements can take root.

The Hypothesis Supported by the Research

The history of gospel music demonstrates continuity in the elements of gospel music with necessary adaptations in an accepted form from the Dorsey to the Franklin Era. As gospel music evolves, so has the social acceptance of what was once controversial in art form, practices, and venue. This has liberated the next generation of gospel artists to have greater opportunity for ministry while leveraging the music industry (Arnold-McFarland A. M., 2016).

The Call to the Aspiring Gospel Artist

This is only a snapshot of the analysis of the evolution, yet the need to bridge the gap between church and industry is urgent. As stated in the conclusion of the book, our worship needs to be able to transcend differences, and even religions, so that it changes the world and makes it a better place. It is urgent that we move forward and face our future with true worshipers who have hope, who are prayerful, and who are better prepared to change the outlook. We need aspiring artists to leverage the industry for this purpose.

Gospel Music One Sound Project

The hope of the Gospel Music One Sound Project is to bring the church music ministry and the gospel music industry into one accord, ONE SOUND, spiritually and in the natural (technically and physically) for kingdom building.

Dr. Antonia Arnold-McFarland
2 Chronicles 5:13–14

Donnie McClurkin's 2011 Perfecting Music Conference, Charlotte, NC

Observation or prescription	Source of Information	Ministry	Industry
The successful gospel artist is effective at creativity, spiritual discernment and maturity, and industry business.	Myron Butler Perfecting Conference 2011	X	X
Ensure legalities for songwriters, collaboration agreements, work-for-hire agreements, copyrights, mechanical licenses, publications, and producers are established before doing any recordings.	Myron Butler Perfecting Conference 2011		X
Understand clearly recorded deal points that translate to pay percentages for producers, artists, songwriters, publishers, and record labels. Understand industry standards for publishing compensation when in contract.	Kerry Douglas, Aaron Lindsey Perfecting Conference 2011		X
The best way for new artists to get on the radio is to get traction by having music on the Internet.	Kerry Douglas, Gary Tom Perfecting Conference 2011		X
Artists can build their artist score through social media technology to gain exposure.	Kerry Douglas Perfecting Conference 2011		X
Provide a good live performance in front of large crowds and have music readily available to sell immediately afterward (megachurches, conferences).	Melanie Clark Israel Houghton Perfecting Conference 2011		X
Life moves at the speed of relationship but not at the speed of opportunity. Great opportunities can follow real relationships. This builds longevity and a legacy.	Aaron Lindsey and Israel Houghton Perfecting Conference 2011	X	
Relationships are the currency of the kingdom. You must be faithful over your local domain before God can trust you with more.	Melanie Clark Perfecting Conference 2011	X	

Observation or prescription	Source of Information	Ministry	Industry
There is a careful balance of business and ministry in gospel music. All artists and industry participants must be very clear and honest with themselves as to why they are seeking a role in the gospel music industry.	Melanie Clark Perfecting Conference 2011	X	
The gospel artist must be able to effectively deliver a good live performance with a testimony that connects with the audience.	Kerry Douglas Perfecting Conference 2011	X	
Each aspiring gospel artist must figure out what it is that gets him or her to that captivating artistic mode.	Conference Concert 2011	X	X
Change the perceptions of musicians in the church by 1) displaying more gratitude, 2) displaying more generosity, 3) having grace, and 4) obtaining godliness from the first three.	Israel Houghton Perfecting Conference 2011	X	

Best Practices for Balancing Ministry in the Industry	**Examples**
1) Demonstrate your mission for the greater good and growth of the kingdom. Demonstrate your conviction for ministry through your spiritual gifting, testimony, charitable cause, or other commission for humanity for training and developing others in ministry to sustain the kingdom. Reference scriptures: James 2: 14–17 Matthew 6:33 Matthew 25:35	Lacrae's Reach Life Ministries: "We want to use the platform we've been given by God to spark a movement of believers that are committed to seeing the gospel saturated in all areas of their life. We are a ministry in its infancy with a commitment to bridging the gap between biblical truth and the urban context." Mahalia Jackson and The Staple Singers used their celebrity to aid in the Civil Rights Movement. Thomas Dorsey started NCGCC, James Cleveland launched GMWA, Edwin and Walter Hawkins launched their Worship and Arts Seminar, Donnie McClurkin hosted a very affordable and informative Perfecting Ministries Conference. Budget time and expense for legitimate charitable/non-profitable causes; concerts that transform lives, assist with disaster relief, or other humanitarian needs. Artist United For Haiti (K. Franklin). Participate in opportunities at your local church or your local community if you do not have your own separate mission. It can be formal or informal until you become established enough to manage it in a more structured manner. The Gospel Music One Sound Project was used for this research but can be leveraged as an ongoing mission for sowing back into developing others for music ministry in the church, community, and industry. The event was funded by donations and personal finance. A cause attached to the event was to collect funds and send a portion of the proceeds to the Salvation Army for the East Coast Floods Effort for the people of South Carolina. As a result, $500 was donated for this special cause. —A. Arnold-McFarland

Best Practices for Balancing Ministry in the Industry	Examples
2) Focus on winning souls instead of on winning sales (K. Franklin). Your platform for music is a method for evangelism in church and non-church venues. Your lifestyle should serve as a role model to win souls, encourage salvation, and encourage the saints. Luke 14:23 Matthew 9:37–38 Matthew 28:18–20 Romans 10:11–15 Philemon 6 Colossians 3:23 Proverbs 16:3	Lacrae offers prayer meetings before NBA games. Kirk Franklin shares his testimony to help others transform their lives, and he has helped bridge sacred and secular artists for ministry purposes. Do not be afraid to cross over into culturally different opportunities. Andrae Crouch, Israel Houghton, BeBe and CeCe Winans, Lecrae, Yolanda Adams, and Mary Mary are just a few artists who have cross- cultural and cross-genre appeal. Roberta Thorpe played gospel music at the Cotton Club to take her music to those who may not attend church. In the 1980s, contemporary group Commissioned provided an altar call in their concerts offering Christ to those who attended.
3) Be accessible and approachable: Stay abreast of practices and technology standards in the industry to make your music ministry accessible and approachable. This also sustains exposure and keeps a pulse on the spiritual needs of people. Exodus 31:1–5 Titus 1:7 2 Timothy 3:17	Numerous gospel artists are now on Periscope, a new social media tool that allows real time tweets and response to followers. Artists are involved in reality TV, have roles as radio personalities, and participate in workshops and seminars for face time with their followers.
4) Learn the business and stay relevant: Acquire knowledge on your own initiative of all aspects of the business of the music industry (copyrights, radio, publishing, recording, contracts, accounting, legalities, artist development, distribution, and promotions). Also study the specifics of the gospel music industry so it can be effectively leveraged as a platform for ministry. Operate your pursuits as a legal business with a trade name and have strategic planning sessions for growth. Maintain your integrity at all times. 2 Timothy 2:15 2 Corinthians 9: 6–7 Luke 16:11 Luke 14:28 Habakkuk 2: 2–3	Increase business acumen via regular and frequent study of trade websites, magazines, and events like the Gospel Music Industry Round Up, Billboard Charts, the Stellar Awards (SAGMA), The Grammy Awards, and musicbizacademy.com. Attend conferences and seminars that provide face time with industry professionals. Understand the legal risks. Join professional organizations (BMI, ASCAP, SESAC) for song protection and to stay informed. See Table 13 as an example of information obtained from Donnie McClurkin's Perfecting Music Conference.

Best Practices for Balancing Ministry in the Industry	Examples
5) Present an art form with sincerity. "Your art form should reflect where you are in your personal spiritual growth with God. If that's not your top priority, then your art form is going to be very shallow. It should not be just for the sole purpose of the art form itself. If it's that, you'll suffer. You have to make sure people can feel the sincerity of your own testimony and your own journey so they know this is something that is really real for you." —K. Franklin. Colossians 3:16 Titus 2:7 Psalm 108:1 John 4:23–24	Thomas Dorsey wrote his most famed composition, "Take My Hand, Precious Lord," out of pain during the lowest point in his life in 1932 upon the news of the death of his wife and child in childbirth. This song became a hymn standard and favorite of Martin Luther King, who requested hearing it sung by Mahalia Jackson. She sang it at his funeral in 1968. Aretha Franklin sang it at Mahalia's funeral in 1972. Leontyne Price sang it at Lyndon B. Johnson's funeral in 1973. It has been recorded by Elvis Presley, Al Greene, Ike and Tina Turner, Andrae Crouch, Pat Boone, BB King, Beyonce, Merle Haggard, and Ledisi, among other notable recordings.
6) Maintain your relationship with God through regular study, practice, and accountability of your Christian faith. Practice your ministry in the local church or community and make time to be ministered to. Balance time between church obligations and your gospel artist pursuits, being careful to not over-commit. Spiritual wellness is a must for ministry and the industry. Spiritual discernment is needed for decisions with sound judgment. It also helps you maintain accountability and humility. Too many musicians get lost to the wayside spiritually because they are so busy working in ministry and not growing from ministry. It is important that your musical message remains biblically sound and theologically accurate. You are accountable for the message you send. Singing or playing for the church or the industry does not guarantee entry to the kingdom. Romans 12:2 Jeremiah 29:11 Revelation 3:20 John 14:6	At the Donnie McClurkin's Perfecting Music Conference in 2011, Israel Houghton talked about how singing is a part of one's worship life. "Sunday is usually the only time we see worship happening. The way we conduct our lives and the way we interact with people is an act of worship. Heart placement is vital to effective worship". He feels compelled to change the perception of many musicians in today's church settings. Musicians can change this perception by focusing on gratitude, generosity, grace and godliness. Also, William Becton stated, "Music ministry leadership must set a standard of sanctification for others to follow and should resist the flesh and carnality, as did the Levites." The scriptural reference for this discussion was 1 Corinthians 1:10 where the apostles teach that as Christians we are to speak the same things and be of the same mind and same judgment without division. This is the expectation for all ministry leadership, including music leaders, as it relates to the vision of the pastor.

Best Practices for Balancing Ministry in the Industry	Examples
7) **Maintain a good reputation and good relationships with genuine people who can mentor you and whom you can influence.** Stay connected with and honor your predecessors. Stay connected with the next generation of artists on the "gospel music continuum" who will stand on your shoulders. Establish and sustain genuine relationships with industry professionals who can mentor your journey. Keep a good reputation in ministry and the industry. This grants favor, and favor is better than riches. Network, support and celebrate others. Romans 15:5–6 Galatians 6:2 Proverbs 22:1	Entry into the gospel music industry is based on skill and relationships. Master your gift and be open to critiques. Dorsey, Cleveland, and Franklin are key examples of artists who made opportunities accessible for others. Established artists mentored and developed up and coming artists. Share your knowledge with those who will come after you. This helps you stay sharp in your own abilities and keeps you relevant with upcoming generations.

References

Arnold-McFarland, A. M. (2015–2017). Gospel Music One Sound Project.

Arnold-McFarland, A. M. (2016). *The evolution of African-American worship: from music ministry to music industry as pursued by the independent gospel artist, from the Thomas Dorsey to the Kirk Franklin Era.* Raleigh, NC: Eflat Major Publishing. Retrieved from https://issuu.com/eflatmajorpublishing/docs/research_project_-_dmin_-_creative_

Perfecting Music Conference. (2011). Donnie McClurkin's Perfecting Music Conference.

Made in the USA
Columbia, SC
24 May 2018